COMPUTER

ORCHESTRATION

Tips and Tricks

Stephen Bennett

PC Publishing

PC Publishing
Keeper's House
Merton
Thetford
Norfolk IP25 6QH
UK

Tel +44 (0)1953 889900
email info@pc-publishing.com
website http://www.pc-publishing.com

First published 2009

© PC Publishing

ISBN 13: 978 1906005 054

British Library Cataloguing in Publication Data
A catalogue record for this book is available from the British Library

Printed and bound in Great Britain by The Cromwell Press Group, Trowbridge, Wilts

Contents

Acknowledgements

I'd like to thank the following – without whose products my orchestral aspirations would have remained unheard.

- Paul Kaufman at IKMultimedia for the Miroslav Philharmonik software (www.ikmultimedia.com).
- Gary Garritan at Garritan for the Personal Orchestra (www.garritan.com).
- Eric Lindemann at Synful for the Synful Orchestra (www.synful.com).
- The Logic development team at Apple.

Introduction

The instruments which go to make up the orchestra have been in use for centuries and the onset of electronic-based popular music has done little to diminish their popularity amongst musicians. Whatever the musical genre, including an orchestral touch will nearly always add a certain 'something' to a recording and, of course, most film scores are still mainly orchestral in nature.

However, to add an orchestra full of 'real' musicians to a track is usually prohibitively expensive for most independent musicians. Even those with recording contracts behind them will often baulk at just how much it costs to hire decent players – not to mention the studio and equipment which you'd need to house and record them. Even recording a small ensemble, for example a string quartet, can be fraught with difficulties. You'll need to provide them with a a readable score along with correct notation. You'll need great players with superb instruments and record them in a fine-sounding room with good quality equipment. And you'll need to have the skills of a conductor to get them to play in exactly the way you desire. So what do you do if you really want to use orchestral textures in your recordings but the aforementioned requirements are beyond your experience, budget or skills? As is often the case, technology can help you out. Creating realistic orchestral Virtual Instruments has been a kind of holy grail amongst music technologists almost from the day that electronic instruments first appeared on the scene. Early instruments, such as the Theremin and Ondes Martenot attempted to simulate the dynamics and timbres available within the orchestral tone palette, and the Mellotron, a tape-based sampling keyboard from the 1950's, paved the way for the digital samplers we know today.

In the last few years, computers have become powerful enough for plug-in Virtual Instruments and soft-samplers to access huge libraries of high-quality orchestral samples. Some of these libraries run to hundreds of gigabytes in disk storage and are extremely costly – though compared to the cost of re-recording a whole orchestra because there's something 'not quite right' in the score, they could be seen as somewhat of a bargain! Film composers regularly use large sample libraries to produce mock-ups of their score which can then can be played to the director and added to a temporary edit of the film – with the advantage that changes can be made easily and the score finalised before any of the expensive recording begins. However, you may not want or need to replace the synthetic orchestra or you might want to use it in conjunction with real players and instruments. Many orchestral libraries are now on the market at several different price points, and even the low-cost ones have excellent sound quality and enough articulations and instruments to make a creditable stab at a realistic orchestra. It's not the purpose of this book to recommend specific products in this rapidly changing market, but to assist you to produce the best results from whichever orchestral library you choose. Although we may refer to specific pieces of software in the book, this is in no way an endorsement of any product. Like many things musical, preferences vary and one person's 'best sound' is another's 'fingers on blackboard'.

One of the main reasons many people are put off even attempting to add or create orchestral simulations in their work is because they feel they can only do so if they have extensive training in what can sometimes be seen as a 'black art', or that they must have an ability to read music. While having some music theory is always a good idea, it is still possible to produce great results with little or no understanding of traditional musical notation. Rather, a good ear and an inquisitive nature will help you create realistic and musical orchestral simulations on your computer. Of course, most modern music software sequencers will also allow you to view and print your creations in traditional notation so, for those wishing to improve their understanding of that area of music, creating your own score can be very inspiring.

What equipment and software do you need?

Although this is almost a kind of 'how long is a piece of string' question, there are several general guidelines which you can follow which should help you choose the correct equipment for your given application.

Computer

Either a laptop or desktop will be suitable – depending on your needs. A large screen can be useful as you'll probably want to display multiple tracks – especially if you are attempting a full orchestral score. Get as fast a processor (CPU) as you can and as much memory (RAM) as you can afford. 32 bit computers can access up to 4GB RAM whereas 64 bit computers and operating systems can access up to 1 Terabyte (1000GB) RAM and many sample libraries allow you to load the samples directly into RAM, thus reducing loading speeds and latency. Multiple core computers are also a good buy as plug-ins are usually very CPU intensive. Basically, the more powerful the computer the more real-time work you'll be able to do and the less you'll have to render or bounce the sounds and parts to hard disk.

Hard drives

If you're using a sample-based orchestral library, a fast (greater than 7200 r.p.m.) disk will greatly improve disk access and loading. Many companies recommend a separate hard disk for storing and loading samples, and external Firewire or USB 2 hard drives are convenient and inexpensive. If you decide to use 24bit versions of the sounds, these will take up about three times the hard disk space of 16bit sounds and put a greater strain on your CPU, so you need to bear that in mind.

Figure 2.1
Yamaha WX5 Wind MIDI controller.

Hardware

You will need some sort of device to enter MIDI note data (a hardware MIDI controller) unless you are going to use the mouse and enter notes one at a time. This could be a traditional keyboard with a MIDI or USB interface, or could be something more exotic such as a wind or percussion controller.

Many libraries allow for the realtime control of performance parameters. So a controller than can output these by wheels, sliders, knobs, pedals or breath control may be useful.

Figure 2.2
Novation Remote SL MIDI controller.

Software

Most Digital Audio Workstations (DAW) will be suitable as long as they are compatible with your chosen orchestral library. Your choice will usually be based on the computer platform you use and the software you favour. As long as you can edit MIDI note and controller data you can use the software to produce orchestral scores. If you want to produce printed scores for other musicians to play you'll need your DAW to have some kind of Score editing facility.

The sounds

Currently, there are two types of ways to obtain realistic orchestral sounds using a computer.

Sample libraries

These are usually recordings of orchestral instruments and are either supplied as raw samples or audio files for loading into your own sampler or as as a dedicated Virtual Instrument which is able to access the supplied library. Usually you will get a full range of instruments, often with separate recordings of different articulations and with and without vibrato. Some libraries come with samples of different bowing or tonguing types and various microphone placements. It's very useful if the Sampler or Virtual Instrument has controls for modifying some performance features, such as bowing, legato or even articulations in real time via MIDI controllers, as this will help with attempting to achieve more natural performances. Some libraries will record each note of an instrument or ensemble with several different articulations, some will only sample a few per octave. As you can imagine, the former technique requires a lot more disk space than the latter and doesn't necessarily mean a better quality library.

Orchestral virtual instruments using software modelling

These use the CPU power of the computer to generate real-time recreations of various orchestral instruments from mathematical models. Samples, while sounding excellent, have a fixed tonal response; they will always sound the same each time they are played back. While sample libraries get around this problem by having different samples play back at different key velocities, this takes up an enormous amount of hard disk space. Software models, on the other hand generate their sounds in real-time and adjust those sounds depending on the player's input and can thus be extremely expressive. However it's a new technology and the software has some way to go before it can compete with the realism of sampled libraries.

Sample rate, bit depth and quality

Sample rates
Higher sample rates, in general, yield higher recording quality. A recording at a given sample rate will yield a recording at half that rate. So 44.1kHz can record up to 22.5kHz – just outside the human hearing range while a 96kHz can record up to 48kHz. However there is a price to pay; higher sample rates require more hard disk space to store the file and more CPU power to process the data. Also, if you plan finally to release your material on audio CD, that format is limited to 44.1kHz – and sample rate conversion is not without its own quality problems. Many libraries are now recorded at extremely high sample rates and which you choose can depend on the final medium in which your work will appear. Which sample rate library you can use may also be dependent on the DAW you are using.

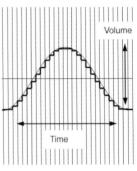

Figure 2.3
Sampled waveform.

Bit depth
The bit depth used in recording defines the resolution and quality of a recording. The lower the bit depth used, the less well an analogue signal will be reproduced, as the recording will use less steps to digitize the sound.

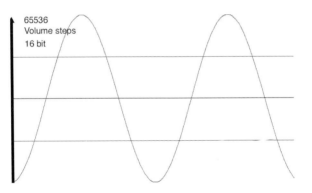

Figure 2.4
16 bit resolution.

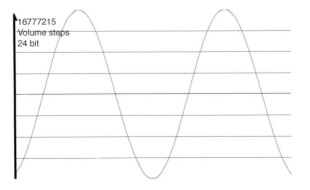

Figure 2.5
24 bit resolution.

Audio CD is a 16 bit medium and it describes 65535 discrete level values. A 4 bit recording system will have only 256. You can look at bit depth in the same way as resolution on a digital camera – the higher the bit depth the more 'in focus' the sound. In audio terms, the bit depth defines the dynamic range, measured in dB. You can measure the dynamic range that will be given by a bit depth using the formula:

6 x the number of bits

So a 16 bit system has a dynamic range of 6 x 16 = 96dB, whereas a 4 bit system has a dynamic range of only 6 x 4 = 24dB

As you can see from the figures above, the greater the bit rate, the more discrete amplitude steps are described by the digitised waveform.

It's possible that libraries recorded at 24 bit resolution will sound better than those recorded at 16 bit, but it's not a foregone conclusion. The venue, the equipment and musicians used for the recording will all impact on the quality of the results and you may choose a library for other reasons, such as the number and type of articulations and and the ease of use. But as mentioned before, there are computer performance issues connected with using higher bit rate recordings, though some libraries allow you to work with 16 bit sounds until the final mix, reducing pressure on the performance of your computer when recording while allowing maximum quality in the final output.

Articulations

We've mentioned articulations several times in this chapter, but what exactly are they? Acoustic instruments, such as those that go to make up the orchestra, are capable of producing a great range of timbres and dynamic styles. When you sample a violin, for example, you capture a 'snapshot' of the playing at that point. The next time the real violinist plays the same note, it may sound completely different. They may bow harder, the attack may be different, they may play an up or down stroke and the loudness and tone may differ from the original recording and may even vary over the duration of the note.

Some of these changes can be emulated using standard audio modifiers such as envelope generators (which control the Attack, Decay, Sustain and Release of the sound – they are sometimes called ADSR for obvious reasons) or the timbre (or tone) can be modified using equalisation and filters, while trills and vibrato can be emulated using Low Frequency Oscillators (LFO). However other changes in playing, such as different bow strokes, pizzicato, spiccato, staccato and a more natural tremolo and vibrato will require separate recordings. So a library may contain recordings of violins playing in many different styles at many different volumes in an attempt to capture more of the natural playing of the instrument. In addition there may be recordings of solo violins and various ensembles playing together (to be used in different applications) – all of which will be recorded playing several articulations. And this is just for a violin – as you can imagine, the number of recordings needed for a ensemble of violinists or complete orchestra can be extremely large!

In addition, some libraries have samples recorded with different micro-phones placed at different positions along with recordings of room ambience which you can blend in with the closely placed microphone recordings to sim-ulate various degrees of room reverberation.

Controllers and using the articulations

With such a wealth of samples available, software companies have come up with various ways for you to access and play the different articulations. Here are a few of the more common methods – though it's by no means an exhaus-tive list. We're using the violin as an example but the examples used here can apply to most instruments.

Key velocity

The MIDI specification allows for a MIDI keyboard to generate velocity values between 0 (silent) and 127 (maximum volume). If you assign different recordings of a violin being played at different velocities to various velocity ranges, the sample that plays back is dependent on how hard you hit the key. A library might also arrange the recordings so that there is more attack and 'bite' as the recordings get louder – just like a real instrument. The Key veloc-ity could also control Envelope generators to adjust attack and duration and filters or EQ to adjust the tone of the sound – which are sometimes user-definable values, so you can experiment with the sounds.

Aftertouch

Aftertouch is generated when you press harder down onto a suitably equipped MIDI keyboard or controller and the MIDI data generated can be used to con-trol articulations or other parameters. For example, pressing a key harder could play samples that have greater and greater amounts of trill or vibrato or could adjust the frequency and depth of a LFO to simulate the same effect.

Modulation (MIDI controller 1)

The modulation wheel is usually used to either control the play back of vari-ous articulations with different vibrato, tremolo or trills or frequency and depth of an LFO to simulate the same effect. Some libraries use this MIDI controller for volume and to create swells and crescendos.

MIDI controllers

Various other MIDI controllers are used in different ways by different libraries.

Volume (MIDI controller 7)

Usually controlled by a pedal, the MIDI data generated can be used to either adjust the level of a single articulation or swap between different articulations at different volumes.

Expression (MIDI controller 11)

Usually controlled by a pedal, the MIDI data generated can be used to either adjust the level and tone of a single articulation or swap between different articulations at different volumes.

Sustain (MIDI controller 64)

Often used to swap between samples of different bow strokes or to allow smooth transitions between notes (legato playing).

Using different notes on the keyboard

Some libraries simply put different articulations on different keys, but as you can imagine this is more useful for those sounds that are un-pitched (such as percussion) or have a small pitch range (so each octave on the keyboard could have a different articulation).

Figure 2.6
Different articulations on different keys.

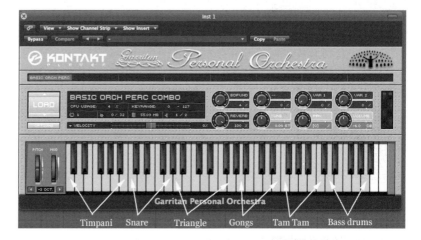

Using KeySwitching

Some libraries reserve the bottom octave or two on a MIDI keyboard for KeySwitching. The way this works is that specific key presses here change which articulation is played back by the rest of the keyboard. For example, pressing low C on the keyboard may allow you to play standard sustained

Figure 2.7
Specific key presses change which articulation is played back by the rest of the keyboard.

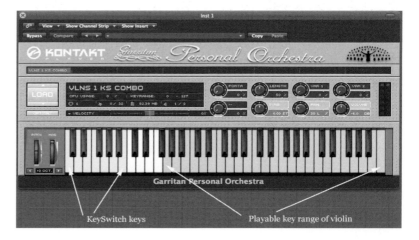

bowing while pressing D changes the sound to pizzicato. Using the DAW, you can record these key presses and thus change sounds on the fly. Using this technique reduces the number of different separate samples or instances of a Virtual Instrument you need to load into the DAW.

Multi timbral sampler Virtual Instrument plug-in

Soft samplers usually allow you to load up to 8 or 16 samples or groups of samples, each controllable from separate MIDI channels. These are then easily accessible for playing.

Figure 2.8
Each sound plays back on a different channel.

However, orchestral simulations usually require more than 16 individual sounds, so you may have to run multiple versions of the same instrument.

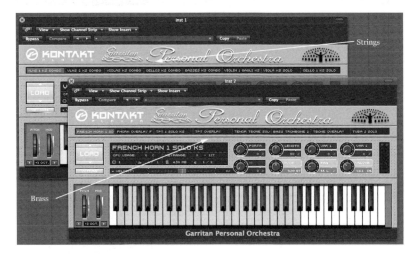

Figure 2.9
Running multiple versions of the same instrument.

Figure 2.10
Load each separate sampler instrument
into its own Virtual Instrument.

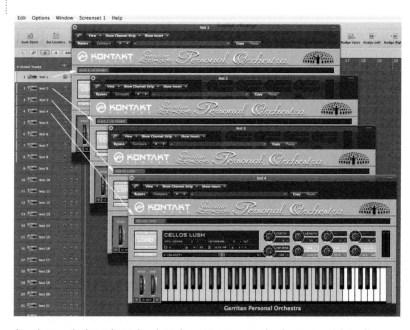

Another technique is to load each separate sampler instrument into its own Virtual Instrument.

Other considerations

Libraries often use separate third-party or or cut-down versions of soft samplers to play back their sounds and the amount of controls and sonic manipulation you can perform on the samples depends on this software. There's been a trend for libraries to be 'locked in' to a dedicated playback program and some are moving towards programs of their own design to allow specific and easier control of the playback of their samples. Increasingly, more visual and automatic methods are being used to help the user create various orchestral ensembles and these are to be welcomed – trying to keep track of hundreds of samples is rather like looking after hundreds of individual musicians and these 'virtual conductors' should become more common in the future.

Conclusions

The choice of software instruments is an extremely personal one – just like the real thing – and may ultimately come down to budget, features and application. If all you're interested in is mocking up a score for real musicians to play or producing a guide for a film director, you won't necessarily need the last word in quality and realism and you might find a simple orchestral library, such as the ones often supplied free with samplers or DAW software, adequate. Generally, the more you pay the more flexibility and sound quality you get – though this is not an absolute rule of thumb. And many great recordings have been made using 'lesser' systems.

What is MIDI ?

MIDI is an acronym for Musical Instrument Digital Interface, so it's a moot point whether a 'MIDI interface' is a tautology or not! Basically, MIDI allows you to control suitably equipped hardware or software synthesisers, effects and mixers via MIDI messages from your computer. These messages range from the most simple, such as telling a synthesiser when to start and stop playing notes, through to more complex control of parameters. Though introduced in the 1980s the 8-bit MIDI standard is still vitally important in technologically based music production and MIDI data messages can be found flying between the various parts of your computer-based music production system as well as being transferred by MIDI interfaces (sic) by USB or the more traditional 5 PIN DIN socket.

MIDI and the synthetic orchestra

How much MIDI information you'll use in your compositions really depends on the orchestral library you are using. Basic libraries may only allow control of simple functions like note on and off, volume, attack and so on, while more sophisticated libraries may allow control of timbre, reverb, legato, release, bowing styles and real-time modification and selection of articulations. Different libraries may use different articulations to perform the same tasks so I'm afraid you're going to have to read the manual of your chosen library if you want to make the best of your orchestral package.

The way it works is like this; when you press a key or move a knob or wheel on a MIDI controller, MIDI data is generated which your orchestral library responds too. The beauty of using a sequencer is that you can record this data and edit it later at your leisure to improve the realism of the performance.

MIDI channels

MIDI data is sent on up to 16 separate MIDI channels. Your orchestral library must be set to receive on the channel you are sending from your MIDI controller for it to respond to your playing.

Multi-timbral MIDI

MIDI data can be sent on multiple channels simultaneously. Many orchestral plug-ins can load several sounds at the same time (violin, violas and so on) and each of these can be set to respond to different MIDI channels. This is efficient in computing power and simplifies the arrangement – having to load 16 instances of your library could get a little complex!

This chapter is a handy guide to which MIDI information does what (usually) with respect to MIDI and orchestral libraries.

Note ON and OFF messages

As their names imply, when your library receives these messages, a note is played and stops playing. Controllers send out MIDI note data when you press a key down and release it. Each key sends out a particular MIDI note number on the channel selected = for example 0 represents C2 and 127 is G8 – plenty enough for an 88 note piano!

Velocity

Controllers often respond to how hard a key is pressed, a note blown, or a string plucked. Possible values are again 0 to 127 with 0 being silence and 127 the maximum. This controller is often mapped to volume (i.e. The harder you hit a key the louder the sound) but can sometimes be used for other purposes.

Aftertouch

Some controllers send out MIDI data when you press down on the keys. This can either be the same amount no matter how many keys are pressed (monophonic aftertouch) or each key can generate its own values depending on the pressure (polyphonic aftertouch).

Pitch bend

Usually controlled by a wheel, knob or ribbon, pitch is usually mapped to the pitch of notes.

Program changes

This is used to change patches on an attached MIDI hardware device or Virtual Instrument – if that instrument accepts program changes.

Controller information

There are 128 controllers defined by the MIDI specification and each can have possible values of 0–127 (are you seeing a pattern here?) Not all orchestral plug-ins can respond to all controllers and not all orchestral libraries respond in the way you'd expect. For example, The Garritan Personal Orchestra uses Controller 1 (Modulation) to control the volume rather than vibrato or tremolo.

Here's a guide to the most common controllers. Note that when the controller is ON/OFF only, its two settings are controlled by MIDI values 0–63 (OFF) and 64–127(ON)

MIDI controllers

Controller no	What it does	What it's used for
1	Modulation	Usually used to add vibrato or tremolo.
2	Breath control	Used to affect the blowing of wind instruments.
5	Portamento	Controls the 'slide' from one note to the next.
7	Volume	Controls overall volume.
8	Balance	Used to set the level of the left and right channel elements of instruments in the stereo field.
10	Pan	Controls the position of an instrument in the stereo field.
11	Expression	This is usually used to control the level of each individual sound in a multi-timbral plug-in with out affecting the overall volume.
12/13	Effects control	Used to adjust the effects available to a plug-in – for example, reverb or chorus.
64	Sustain pedal ON/OFF	In pianos, used to turn the sustain on and off. In other libraries can control the legato or bowing settings.
65	Portamento ON/OFF	Only turns off the level set by controller number 5.
66 the	Sostenuto ON/OFF	Similar to the sustain controller but but only holds notes that were present when pedal is pressed.
67	Soft pedal ON/OFF	Lowers the volume of notes played.
68	Legato ON/OFF	Controls the legato effect in some libraries
69	Hold ON/OFF	Similar to sustain but notes fade according to their own sustain settings.
70-74	Sound controllers	Usually mapped to synthesiser functions such as oscillator waveform settings, fil ters, envelope generators and so on.
75-79	Sound controllers	Use depends on the library used.
80-83	General purpose controllers ON/OFF	Similar to above but just used to switch controls on and off.
91-95	Effects depth	Used to control the level of effects such as reverb or echo.

Unused controllers up to 95 are often put to use in various libraries for different tasks.

Controllers 96-127 are specialised controllers and are not usually used by plug-ins to adjust and control sounds.

Working with MIDI data

Though the descriptions detailed earlier in the chapter may seem like gobbledygook to those unused to Digital Audio Workstations (DAW), MIDI sequencers and other MIDI hardware and software, as with many things, it's often harder to write about them than actually to use them. So we'll take some 'real world' examples of the use of MIDI data with the synthetic orchestra.

Of course, this information can be used to edit any MIDI data, not just that relating to orchestral libraries – which are actually just specialised versions of 'common' Virtual Instruments.

If you press a key on a MIDI controller keyboard and record the input the result will look something like Figure 3.1 if displayed in the DAW's text or list editor.

Figure 3.1

The different columns specify various parameters related to the inputted data. These may differ depending on your DAW but most of these parameters will usually be listed. Here's what they mean;

Position
This is the position in the timeline of the song where the note occurs.

Status
This describes what type of MIDI data it is.

Channel (Ch)
This is the MIDI channel the data is on.

Num
If the data is a note, this shows the actual note.

Val
The value of the velocity information – i.e. how hard you hit the key.

Length
How long the data lasts for. If it's a note, the length of the note.

As you can see, it's easy to micromanage your MIDI data precisely using these kinds of List editors.

Now let's add some volume swells using the Expression controller (MIDI controller 11) – which could be entered by the mouse or via a MIDI controller (a foot pedal for example).

You can see (Figure 3.2) that the line which shows the expression swell is shown as several discrete points. The curve could actually be drawn on a

Figure 3.2

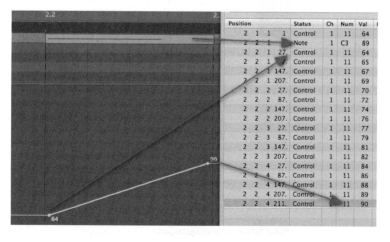

graph with the Volume data as the Y axis and the position as the X axis, as shown in Figure 3.3.

Now we add some Vibrato via the Modulation MIDI controller (number 1) – which could be drawn in using the mouse or entered via a hardware controller – usually the modulation wheel on a MIDI controller (Figure 3.4).

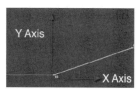

Figure 3.3

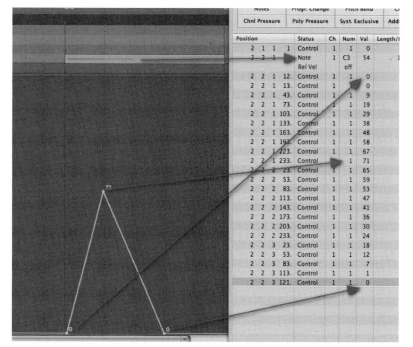

Figure 3.4

Finally (Figure 3.5) we can add a sustain pedal MIDI controller (number 64). In some orchestral libraries, this can be used to change articulations, for example.

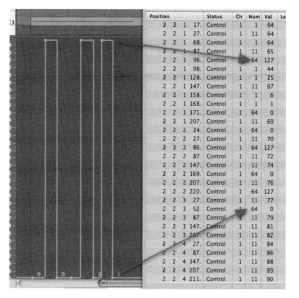

Figure 3.5

Note that this controller is used in an 'on and off' fashion and is usually entered using a footpedal. In MIDI parlance, 0 is OFF while 127 is ON.

Some MIDI data is defined as values 0-127. For example, if you are controlling the attack of a sample, 0 could be the fastest attack and 127 the slowest (Figure 3.6).

Figure 3.6

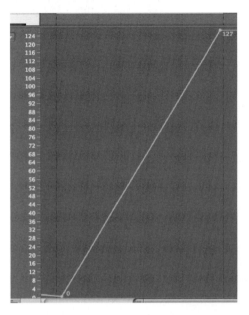

Some data is defined as + and – 64. For example, using pitch bend data, a value of 0 is no pitch change while positive values define a pitch change upwards while negative values define downward pitch changes (Figure 3.7).

Figure 3.7

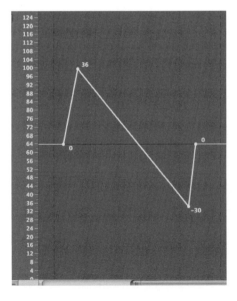

Some data is defined as on or off. For example, a switch for changing string part bowing positions from up or down could be defined by 0 as bowing up and 127 as bowing down.

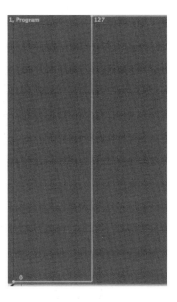

Figure 3.8

Note: MIDI is an 8-bit system so it is limited to 127 discrete steps. This may seem like a limitation (a 16-bit system would allow 65535 discrete steps, for example), but it is usually enough to define and control a Virtual Instrument's parameters.

The orchestra and its synthetic equivalent

The orchestra contains many individual instruments which combine to make up a composite sound. You may want to emulate anything from a small ensemble, say a string quartet or wind group, right up to a full orchestra, so you'll need to choose a library with enough articulations and instruments to cover your requirements. This chapter outlines the instruments of the orchestra – but it's by no means an exhaustive list. Composers have, over the years, augmented the traditional instrumentation with other sounds, so if you want to add a Theremin or E-Bow guitar to your scores don't feel you have to be restricted to the instruments in this chapter.

Articulations

Acoustic instruments can be played in many ways. For example, a violin can be bowed quickly or slowly, with or without vibrato. You can scrape the bow across or bounce the bow on the strings, pluck them with your fingers and so on. You can also do some less obvious things with a violin. You can tap the body, drum your fingers on it and even smash it into little pieces if you so desire! Some libraries can contain all these so-called articulations, including tuning up samples, while some contain just the basics.

The numbers of instruments and samples in any orchestral setup can vary quite widely depending on the cost of the library and its intended use. Some libraries provide samples of ensembles while some may allow you to add together solo recordings to form an ensemble.

Instruments of the orchestra

Strings

All string instruments can produce the following useful articulations:

Staccato – short notes with plenty of space between them.
Legato – notes are connected but with a defined break between the notes.
Sustain – notes held for longer durations
Pizzicato – plucking of the strings
Mutes – as the name implies, a muted tone
Trills – stepping between pitches rapidly
Tremolo – volume modulation
Vibrato – pitch modulation
Up and down bowing

Violin

Used traditionally as:

Solo
Ensembles

Viola

Used traditionally as:

Ensembles

Cello

Used traditionally as:

Solo
Ensembles

Bass

Used traditionally as:

Ensembles

Woodwinds

All woodwinds can have the following useful articulations:

Sustained blowing
Tonguing – short bursts of air into the instrument

Piccolo

Used traditionally as:

Ensembles
Solo

Concert flute

Used traditionally as:

Ensembles
Solo

Alto flute

Used traditionally as:

Ensembles
Solo

Bass flute
Used traditionally as:

Ensembles

Oboe
Used traditionally as:

Ensembles
Solo

English horn
Used traditionally as:

Ensembles
Solo

Eb clarinet
Used traditionally as:

Ensembles
Solo

Bb clarinet
Used traditionally as:

Ensembles
Solo

Bass clarinet
Used traditionally as:

Ensembles

Contrabass clarinet
Used traditionally as:

Ensembles

Bassoon
Used traditionally as:

Ensembles
Solo

Contra bassoon
Used traditionally as:

Ensembles

Brass

French horn
Used traditionally as:

Ensembles
Solo

Trumpet
Used traditionally as:

Ensembles
Solo

Trombone
Used traditionally as:

Ensembles
Solo

Bass trombone
Used traditionally as:

Ensembles

Tuba
Used traditionally as:

Ensembles
Solo

Percussion
Percussion instruments in the orchestra are slightly different from the other instruments and also from their rock or jazz based counterparts. Usually each percussion piece will be played as individual instruments rather than as a 'kit'. Depending on the size of the orchestra, you may have several players concentrating on one or two instruments separately.

Timpani
Snare drum
Bass drum
Cymbals
Triangle

Wood block
Tambourine
Marimba
Xylophone
Glockenspiel
Gong

Keyboard instruments

Most keyboard instruments play a backing-type role in the orchestra unless the piece features the particular instrument, such as a piano concerto for example.

Harp
Celeste
Piano
Harpsichord
Pipe organ

Instrument note ranges

In this section we'll refer to the notes produced by instruments by referring to the range of a standard 5 octave MIDI keyboard. The MIDI specification defines notes as numbers with 0 being the lowest C on your keyboard (if it goes that low) and middle C being 60. You can usually see the MIDI note number being generated when you press a key in your software or you can use one of the free utilities to display incoming MIDI data – see Appendix 2 The Internet.

Info

The ranges and note numbers described in this section may differ from your MIDI keyboard, but you should be able to transpose the information to your particular MIDI controller.

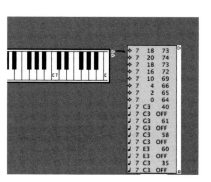

Figure 4.1

Orchestral instruments have pitch ranges defined by their physical layout and, to some extent, the expertise of the player. For example, a trumpet has a theoretical range of range of notes from G2 (MIDI note 55) to Bb4 (MIDI note number 82). However the highest and lowest notes are usually only playable by the finest players and some scores reflect this.

Instrument range diagrams

Figure 4.2
Pitch and MIDI note ranges of strings
and brass orchestral instruments.

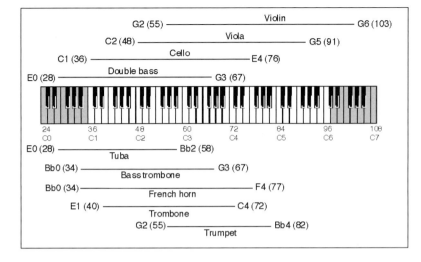

Figure 4.3
Pitch and MIDI note ranges of orchestral
percussion instruments.

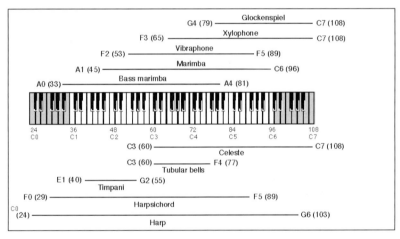

Figure 4.4
Pitch and MIDI note ranges of orchestral
woodwind instruments.

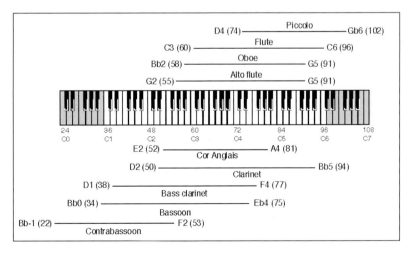

Because the orchestra has evolved naturally over the years, it has incorpo-rated instruments that naturally sound good when blended together. For example while the violin's lower register overlaps somewhat with the viola the two basically have quite distinct note ranges. The same is true with many other instruments. If you've ever tried to mix a rock or pop track, you'll know that it's sometimes difficult to get the vocals, guitars and keyboards to sit well together. This is because the sounds might all be occupying the same fre-quency range and are all competing for the same aural space. Usually, you need to use EQ to sculpt out or boost certain frequencies in each instrument to give each one space to breathe. The orchestra is, in effect, self-mixing. The basses play the bass, the violins the high parts and the others sit in their nat-ural places.

Timbre

Each type of orchestral instrument also has a distinct timbre (or tone) and again are chosen to complement each other. Violins, violas and cellos will blend togeth-er naturally without recourse to equalisation. The brass will blend together too and be distinct from the strings, which in turn is distinct from the woodwind.

Position and number of players

When you go and see an orchestra or a string quartet live you'll notice that the musicians will almost always be spread out on the stage in the same way each time. This isn't done because of tradition or just to fit everyone on the stage – the position of each musician has evolved over the years for some very good reasons. Different instruments in the orchestra have different loud-ness levels and the layout helps to make sure that the individual sections can be clearly heard. You only have to hear a trumpet and piccolo playing to realise these instruments have very different maximum loudness levels! It's not really possible to get musicians just to play more quietly as this may affect the timbre of the instrument or the feel of the performance. So orchestras solve this problem in two different ways.

Position

Figure 4.5 shows the 'standard' layout of the orchestra. As you would expect, the louder instruments are placed at the back (percussion and brass) while

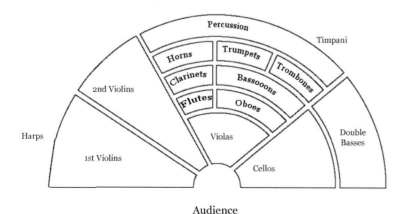

Figure 4.5
The standard layout of the orchestra

Tip

Some samples are recorded in stereo and the position of the individual instrument is 'locked' into place in the stereo image – this makes it easy to set the correct positioning and probably should not be changed using the Virtual Instrument pan control.

the quieter instruments are spread across the sound stage at the front. There's also a timbral element here; the higher pitched strings, which could clash with the flutes are moved out to the left while the woodwinds are allowed to sing out over the violas. The layout of smaller ensembles is less strict and you'll find a wide range of positioning traditions. Of course, with the synthetic orchestra you can use your panning and balance controls to place the instruments where you want; however, if you are looking to create realistic scores, it's sensible to use 'traditional' positioning wherever you can.

Number of players

An orchestrator will try and balance the elements of the orchestra by adjusting the number of players in each section. Though a trumpet may be louder than a violin, it might struggle against 22 of the stringed beasties! Most libraries' sections are recorded as groups of players and depending on the software, you may be able to choose from different numbers of players in each section for a mix 'n match approach.

Tip

If you want to 'double up' sections, i.e. have two sections of the same instrument playing together, don't use the same sample twice as this can lead to tone and phasing problems. Some libraries offer different recordings of the same sections or you can even use a second library for the 'doubled' section.

The basics of orchestration

While this book is aimed at helping get the novice to produce realistic orchestral results, what it doesn't try to be is a comprehensive guide to orchestration. As you can imagine, this subject is one that could take a lifetime of study and people more qualified people than I have written major treatises on the subject. These including composers as diverse as Rimsky-Korsakov and Henry Mancini.

Info

Appendix 2 – The Internet has some links to online guides to orchestration, and while these are heavy on the music theory, they may be of interest if your appetite is whetted by this book.

Do I need to read and write traditional music notation to produce successful orchestrations?

Traditionally, writing music for the orchestra has meant you needed to be pretty hot with a thorough understanding of music notation. This is because you'd have had to manually write the music down (or get someone else to do it for you if you were rich enough!) for the musicians to play. Using a computer means that you don't need to do this any more – unless you want real musicians to play your score. But even then, the computer can help you to produce a printed traditional notation score. However there are certain things you'll need to bear in mind if you're going to do this. These are covered in Chapter 9. So the short answer is no, you don't need to 'read the dots ' to create realistic orchestral simulations. But you do need to understand a bit about how a traditional orchestrator will put together a score.

What is orchestration?

The dictionary definition of orchestration is 'to arrange or direct the elements of (a situation) to produce a desired effect' and that's exactly what is needed when producing a score. The composer directs the elements (instruments) to produce the desired effect (the music). It refers specifically to the orchestra – you would probably use the term 'arranging' for more conventional band-based music. Although the orchestra consists of many discrete instruments, it is, for all intents and purposes, a single instrument – usually 'played' by a conductor. In the world of computer-based orchestration, you take the place of the conductor, the DAW becoming your bow. Though the term is usually applied to large ensembles, orchestration can also refer to pieces written for smaller groups of musicians made up of traditional orchestral instruments. It's a flexible term, but what we are usually talking about in this book is creating simulations of orchestral recordings, both large and small.

Where to begin

At first glance, writing music for the orchestra looks like an enormous task, weighted down by years of history. Its scholarly appearance and the fact that, in the past, the chances of actually hearing your work performed by an orchestra (or even a good small ensemble) was practically nil. But if you look at the orchestra in a similar way to a multi-timbral synthesiser, things become a little less daunting. A multi-timbral synthesiser or workstation can produce different sounds which are then played back on different MIDI channels. You could, for example, have a bass sound playing on channel 1, piano on 2, organ on 3 and drums on 4, for example. You wouldn't play all these sounds together; most likely you'd lay out the drums first, add the bass then piano and so on until you build up a complete song. If you imagine an orchestra like this, breaking it down into its constituent parts, then things become a lot easier to handle.

Avoiding problems

Many Virtual Instruments and synthesisers have presets with names like 'strings' or 'Full Orchestra' and it's tempting to play these sounds using the type of chords you may use when playing a piano. Usually, while the results may sound quite nice, they'll be disappointing in the orchestral sense – they'll sound nothing like a real orchestra no matter how realistic a single note may sound. This is because a real orchestra doesn't work in this way. Let's take a simple triad – a chord with three notes – say C, E and G. If you play this on a piano or organ the same sound will play all notes. However, in an orchestra the violins may play the G, the Violas the E and the Cellos the C. In addi-

Figure 5.1

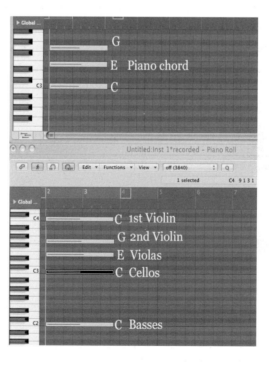

tion, the notes may not be clustered in the same octave as on a piano, they may be spread over a larger range. When you play a chord on the piano, all the notes usually stop and start at the same time and have a similar dynamic range. When you have a chord played by different players or groups of players, they have great flexibility in these areas. You may double up the C on the basses or get the violins to play the C as you want this to be the prominent note (Figure 5.1).

Let's looks at another example. If you write a simple chord sequence and melody like Figure 5.2 ...

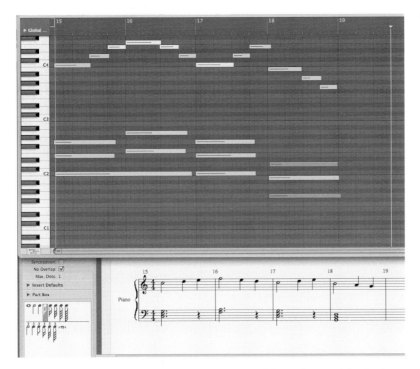

Figure 5.2

and play it using a 'string' preset on a keyboard it won't sound in the least like an orchestra. But if you split the parts as in Figure 5.3...

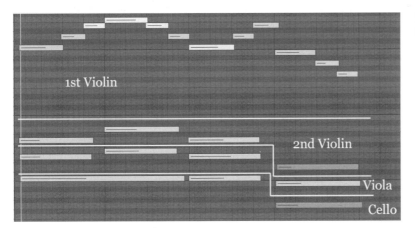

Figure 5.3
Split the parts to improve realism

and assign each part to the 'correct' samples, you'll hear that it's already sounding more 'orchestral' in nature. Of course, there's a long way to go before it'll fool a listener into believing they are listening to a bunch of musicians scraping their bows and blowing their trumpets, but it's a start and illustrates that orchestration isn't rocket science; it uses the same notes as other musical forms and in many cases the same instruments. If you keep in mind that an orchestra is like a single instrument but made up of many individual players, you're well on your way to understanding why it sounds the way it does and how to recreate that sound using samples.

Improving your orchestrating skills

Like any instrument, you can't expect to just load up an orchestral library plug-in, select a few sounds, play a few notes. and everything will come out sounding perfect. As you're reading this book, I assume you have some skill in song arranging, production or recording so you'll realise that you'll have to treat the skill of orchestration in the same way that you had to do with any other of your talents. This means you have to tackle the following areas:

- Understanding articulations and how best to use the orchestral instrumental palette.
- Knowing the physical position of the individual instruments of the orchestra.
- Knowing what each individual instrument can and cannot achieve.
- Knowing how to fit in this knowledge alongside the other parts of the composition.

Fit the score around the song

As mentioned earlier, a large part in getting the orchestration to fit into a song is to make sure the arrangement works well. If you want to feature the orchestral score, make it prominent in parts where other instruments, such as vocal or guitar, are not. If you want strings to wash and support a chorus, use muted timbres so they don't overwhelm the other instruments. Most pop music contains a bass guitar, so you may wish to limit, or omit altogether, the orchestral bass instruments so they don't clash. As is so often the case in music, simpler is often better. A section using samples of violins, violas, and cellos may give you just enough orchestral 'flavour' without needing to add the whole panoply of brass, woodwinds and percussion.

Listen, listen and listen!

It really pays to listen to a lot of music which has orchestral additions. I'd recommend setting up a playlist on an MP3 player or a mix CD of tracks which contain similar performances to the ones you wish to emulate to see how other people go about the business. Appendix 2 has an Internet link where you'll find some 'suggested tracks' for you to listen to. The more you listen to real musicians playing real orchestral instruments, the more you'll get an idea of how to go about trying to emulate these performances in software.

Soccer balls

Even when a real string section is playing simple three or four part chords, you'll notice that they hardly ever change notes exactly at the same time. In addition, there will often be small flourishes to and from the notes to add a little movement and interest to the piece. Orchestral musicians call dull boring blocks of notes 'football music'. Ideally each part should appear as an interesting melody in its own right. But don't make them too complicated otherwise they'll interfere with the song's main theme.

Slurring

No, not the effects of the lunchtime alcohol on musicians, but the common practice for orchestral musicians to move from one note to the next without having a definite break in between – on those instruments which allow it, such as strings and brass.

Realistic slurring is hard to fake – the best method is to use the slur articulations from your library (if you have them). However, these may not fit the style and tempo of the piece you are working on, so you may have to use the Pitch Bend MIDI Controller to sweep up between notes. Accurate pitch bending using a wheel on your master keyboard isn't easy, so I'd recommend adding in the data manually.

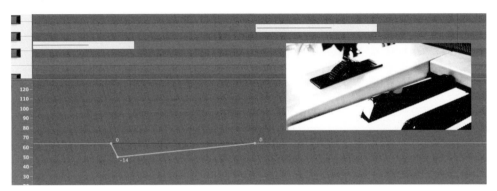

Figure 5.4
Use Pitch Bend to sweep up between notes.

Think real

For maximum realism, it's as well to be aware of the limitations of the players themselves. The range of the notes which the instruments can play has been mentioned, but there are other issues to consider. Certain note transitions are easier on a flute than others – which is why you'll often come across the same runs and trills again and again in music. String players have four strings to play with – and it may not be easy for them to jump to the same notes you have your virtual orchestra playing. As you can imagine, with only four fingers to use, playing five fast notes in row may be beyond all but the most talented!

Adding extra colours

Of course, we are talking tonal colour here, and there are many ways to augment the basic string, woodwind, percussion and brass parts used when scoring. Here are a few ideas to get you started.

- Add a flute or piccolo doubling up or harmonising with the high string parts to make these sing out more.
- If you are creating a crescendo (a swell up to a big 'dah dah!'), add a harp swirl along with the other instruments and a cymbal crash at the end. If you want it to be really dramatic, add in some tympani as well! Xylophones, glockenspiels and bells can all add mystery or drama to a piece, and instruments like cowbells and woodblocks can be useful if you really have decided that comedy songs are coming back into style.

Know your instruments

There's absolutely no point in trying to recreate a realistic orchestral score if you are not going to play each synthetic instrument in a similar fashion to a real one. The pitch range issues have been covered, but there are other important limitations to be aware of.

Strings

Though it's usual for a player to play single notes it is possible to play two note chords on these instruments. But this is limited by combinations which can be played on adjacent strings. Each string on a violin can cover about an octave depending on the skill of the player.

Brass

Brass instruments are monophonic – i.e you can play only a single note at a time – unless you are extraordinarily skilled in playing harmonics along with the fundamental! As they do not have keys, notes will almost always be slurred if played in a legato style. Polyphonic playing is usually done in ensembles, either several of the same or different instruments playing the individual parts.

Woodwind

Woodwinds are monophonic and have keys which accurately define the pitch. However, skilled clarinet players can use reed pressure to bend notes, and oboes and flutes do have some flexibility in this area when in the hands of good players. Because of their keying, some note transitions will always be easier to play than others. Polyphonic playing is usually done in ensembles, using either several of the same or different instruments playing the individual parts.

Other instruments

Harp – generally the harp plays discrete notes, but it has a very distinctive style when 'strummed'. Many libraries use MIDI files (predefined files of notes) to simulate this effect whilst others have samples of harps in different keys and played at different speeds of strum. The advantage of the former is that these MIDI files can be edited in pitch and tempo and fitted exactly into a piece – but the samples of a performance will nearly always sound more realistic.

Pitched percussion (Glockenspiel, Timpani, Tubular bells, Marimba, Xylophone etc.) – will often use MIDI controller data to produce a dampened version of the sound. The Vibraphone may also add a MIDI controller to adjust the tremolo sound from its electric resonators.

Harpsichord – you can often use Key Switching or MIDI controllers to adjust the stop settings to modify the tone.

The instruments – some extra useful tips

String harmonics

These are overtones of the fundamental pitch that can be made to sound louder than the root note by experienced players. Many sample libraries contain harmonic samples and these can produce an eerie thin tone, either one or two octaves above the fundamental, or a harmony, such as the perfect fourth – which is a C note generated by the open G string of the violin.

Violin playing limitations

Violins are tuned GDEA from the lowest string to the highest in pitch, the G being the one in the third octave below middle C on the piano. This makes certain two note chords impossible to play together so you need to bear this in mind when writing for solo strings. Of course, there is nothing to stop you using two different violins to create the chord! When creating your score, you need to be aware that a movement from G to F on the G string can easily be done using slurs and portamento, while changing strings will often cause a sharper, more sudden attack. If you remember these little details and apply them when composing, it will add to the realism of a part.

Other string instrument limitations

Viola
The viola is tuned to CGDA, the C being the one in the third octave below middle C on the piano and has similar limitations to the violin albeit with differing notes due to the different tuning.

Cello
The cello is tuned to CGDA but an octave below the viola and has similar limitations to the violin albeit with differing notes due to the different tuning.

Double bass
The double bass is tuned to EADG but an octave below the cello and has similar limitations to the violin albeit with differing notes due to the different tuning.

Woodwinds
Flutes are quite capable of jumping an octave or more between consecutive notes. Flutes are pretty quiet instruments, so making a single flute louder than the other instruments can sound odd – unless it's a specific effect you are after. Clarinets are also quite capable of jumping an octave or more between consecutive notes, but perhaps it's not as easy as it is on the flute. Clarinet players often use slurs and rarely use vibrato in orchestral music.

The physically larger the woodwind, the less agile the parts the player is likely to be able to play, so avoid ultra-fast runs on the bassoon!

Brass instruments

General considerations
If you've ever tried to play a brass instrument, each 'parp' takes a finite amount of time and requires considerable physical effort. This means that fast runs are difficult and often avoided in orchestral music.

Glissandos and slides are easy to play on brass instruments working, as they do, by adjusting the length of a pipe using a valve. Higher pitched brass

Info

The cello and double bass parts often play exactly the same parts but an octave apart. In pop orchestrations, the basses (and occasionally the cellos) are omitted so as not to clash with the bass guitar.

are much more agile instruments, so fast parts are more likely to be written for the piccolo trumpet than the tuba.

Tone controls

Brass instruments have quite a wide range of tones, with trumpets being bright and the French horn having a mellow melancholic sound.

Mutes

Brass players often use mutes to block up the end of the bell and prevent wind and sound escaping. Different mutes produce different tones and libraries may offer a choice. Mutes make even the most strident brass sound mellow.

Breath/wind controllers

Using a dedicated breath or wind controller that generates MIDI controller data can really add realism to brass parts. Basically, these (depending on the model) can produce MIDI data from blowing velocity and tonguing and this data can then be used to control various parameters of your library's plug-ins, such as timbre, attack and velocity.

Scoring in the sequencer

Producing a realistic orchestral recording means you need to use several techniques to achieve the results you are after – all of which are covered in this and forthcoming chapters. For convenience, we can split these into the following sections:

Choosing the sounds and articulations
This is dealt with in this chapter.

Entering the note data into the MIDI sequencer or DAW
This is dealt with in Chapter 7.

Editing the note data
This is dealt with in Chapter 7.

Mixing the results into a coherent whole and producing a final product
This is dealt with in Chapter 8. However, you will find yourself swapping between these sections as the composition progresses. For example, you may find yourself changing sounds and editing parts right up to the mixdown.

Getting started

Like many things in life, if you plan out what you want to do in advance, it'll be much easier to obtain the results you want later on. The examples we are going to use in this chapter cover tonal music – that is music using the 12 note scale and themes, melodies and rhythms – though there's no reason why you can't produce Stockhausen-like results if you so desire! Many composers like to start with a simple score, with either just a melody or with a piano accompaniment and then flesh out the basics of the part as the song progresses. This could be anything from a section of a traditional song you want to augment or a complete piece for orchestra.

When you are writing parts for orchestra there are a few things you need to bear in mind which are covered below. These aren't really too complicated; this book assumes you have some experience in creating music as songs or instrumentals, so you already have the basic skills needed. It's sometimes hard to get over the weight of hundreds of years of history which orchestration bears with it, but if you look at an orchestra as just a really, really big instrument things will start to seem a little less daunting.

The arrangement

If you've ever done any mixing you'll know that a well arranged song will almost mix itself while a badly arranged song usually requires a lot of remedial work to sound right – even if that's possible at all. If you listen to classic songs by the likes of Burt Bacharach, they often sound somehow 'just right'. But there's no studio trickery involved here – it's all in the arrangement. At its basic level, arranging is getting the parts of the song, the chorus, verse, bridge and so on in the right order. Then you need to look at dynamics and tension within the song and finally, which instruments will fit in with your ideas. I try and look at a piece of music having the following components; time (what happens over the song's duration), frequency (what instruments fill the frequency range) and amplitude (the dynamics). If you start to think of which instruments will fill up the frequency range in a complementary fashion when you are writing your piece, you'll have fewer problems later on. If you try and sit some orchestral colour over a previously recorded track which originally didn't sport it and which already has a full arrangement, it will always be harder to work on than something that has had space left for the orchestra in right from the start.

In this example I've written and recorded a simple piece which I want to orchestrate. This won't win me any awards as a composer, but it's just enough to give you an idea of the steps needed to produce successful results. Here's the piece displayed in the piano roll editor of my DAW sequencer and is played back using a basic piano sound. A piano is useful in these cases as the instrument is open, dynamic and it's easy to produce a melody line and accompaniment that will sound pretty good on its own. It also covers a similar note-range to a full orchestra.

Figure 6.1
A simple piano melody

As you can see, I've recorded a simple melody line (lead) with a basic triad-based chordal backing. Now you don't need to be able to play keyboards to do this – not only do you not need to be fluent in traditional notation to produce orchestral simulations, you don't need to be able to play anything either! You can use your DAW's step time input to add notes – or play in the parts as best you can and then use the DAW's MIDI editing and quantization facilities to produce something that sounds in time and with the right notes. It's OK not to bring the notes into strict time at the moment – better in fact as we'll add the 'human' feel later! You may also want to make sure there are no note overlaps at this stage either, as we're dealing mostly with monophonic instruments here – usually only one note at a time can be played unless you're really trying to emulate players who are good at generating harmonics.

As you can see from Figure 6.1, all the notes are grouped together into the same part. So first we'll need to separate these out to get them to play different orchestral instruments. On some DAWs you can click on notes or a series of notes and define the MIDI channel they will play back on. But for clarity in our example, we'll split out the notes out into separate regions. Some DAWs will let you highlight the notes you want and create new regions on new tracks automatically while with others you'll need to highlight the notes and cut and paste them into new regions.

Figure 6.2

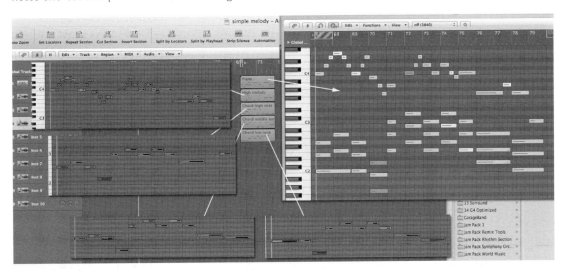

Once we have the notes out, we can get them to play back orchestral instruments instead of the piano. There are two ways to do this, depending on your orchestral library software. You can either use one instance of a multi-timbral plug-in and send each track to the respective inserted sounds (Figure 6.3).

Info

Each track must have its MIDI channel set to the same one as the sound you wish to use on your Virtual Instrument.

Figure 6.3

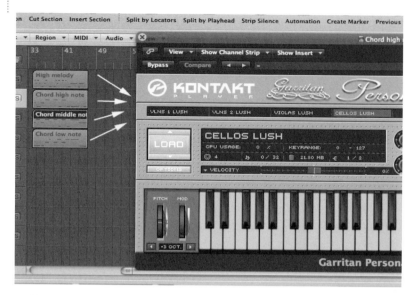

Or you can instance a separate instrument on separate tracks (this method can require more CPU power than using a multi-timbral plug-in.

Figure 6.4

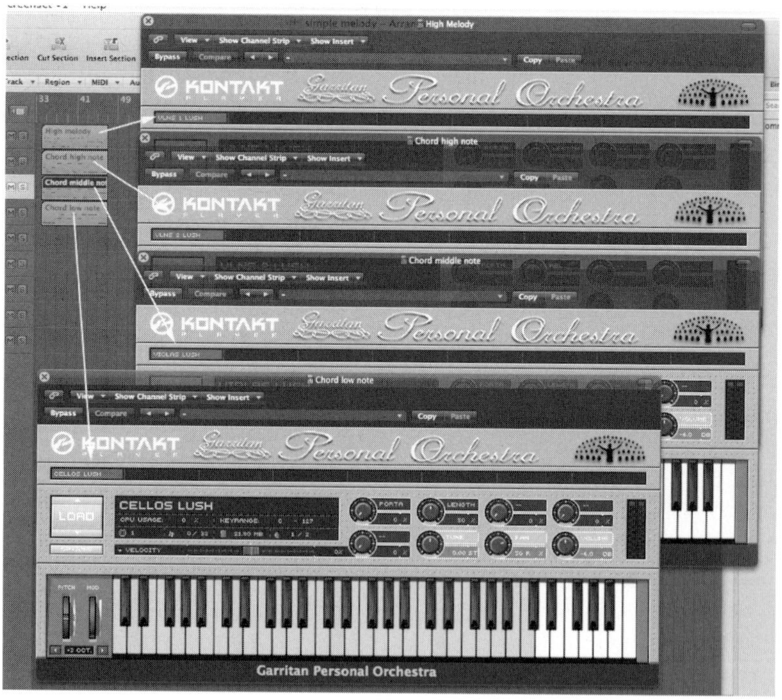

Now we have a violin ensemble playing the lead melody, a viola ensemble playing the top line of the chord, cellos playing the middle line and basses playing the low notes. Initially, you should choose ensemble-type sounds with a long sustain for this.

Because they were played close together, the notes will not be in the correct range for the orchestral samples (see Chapter 5 for more on this). So let's change this using the DAW's transpose facilities. In this example I've brought the cellos down an octave (12 semitones). This has the added advantage, of course, of adding bottom end to the sound. Note that one of

Figure 6.5

the low piano notes is actually too low for the cello sample to play (and thus a real cello), so this will need to be edited.

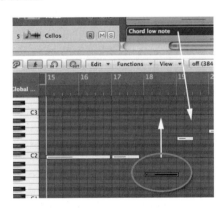

Figure 6.6

By now you should hear that the piece is already sounding better – try changing the piano sound playing the original melody to a generic 'strings' or 'orchestral' sound and comparing the results with your 'orchestrated' version.

In a real orchestra, the parts would be played by individual people who won't play perfectly together in time. If you use your sequencer's MIDI editor to move the notes around a little, it will increase the realism of your parts.

Some programs have a 'humanise' function (Figure 6.7) which applies a randomness to selected note's position and velocity (and thus, usually, timbre). This can also help to make the part sound more like it was played by humans rather than a computer.

Though what we have so far is starting to sound like it wasn't played from a keyboard, it's still a little dull. Real players would find these chords pretty boring to play and it's rare for a real orchestration to be so rigid. The more like a proper arrangement you can emulate, the more realistic your synthetic orchestra will sound.

Tip

Don't over-quantize! Quantization – the process of rigidly bringing the notes on to a specified beat – is the kiss of death when trying to simulate realistic orchestral parts.

Figure 6.7
'Humanise' applies a randomness to a
selected note's position and velocity

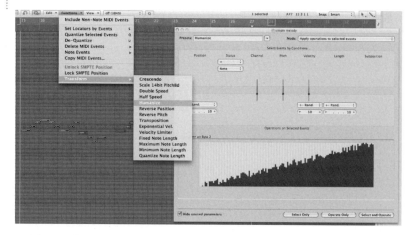

Tip

Don't use the same samples as
the first violin or when
doubling up parts. Using a
different set of samples will avoid
phase and other issues which may
cause the part to sound less
powerful.

Most orchestral music has two violin sections called first and second. The
first usually plays the lead melody and the second either a double, harmony
or counterpoint. So let's change the second violin part and assign it to a copy
of the first violin part. Use your DAW cut and paste facilities to copy the part.

Figure 6.8

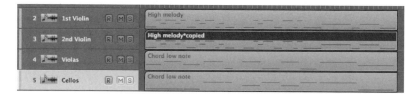

Assign this part to be played by a second violin section.

Now add some weight to the sound by copying the cello part to a new
Track, transpose it down an octave and add a double bass to the virtual
instrument to play the new part.

Figure 6.9

A bit about the frequency spectrum

Human hearing ranges from about 20Hz to 20kHz. However, you'd be hard pressed to find someone over the age of thirty who can hear the higher range of frequencies from 15-20khz and the lower range, 30-70Hz are often not reproduced by most playback systems. To the range in between, the other instruments which make up a track need to be squeezed.

Some, such as bass and bass drum, will occupy the lower range, while cymbals and violins will occupy the upper frequency range. In the past, an arranger would put together a group of instruments that had complementary frequency ranges so that mixing would simply be a matter of balancing the levels of the instruments. It's a 'rule' that still has some validity today. If you try and put together instruments that have clashing frequencies you may have problems making them heard in the mix without resorting to equalisation or other studio trickery that may affect the tonal qualities of the instruments.

Typical string section layouts

Usually, a string section will be made up of first and second violins, violas, cellos and double basses.

Adding some orchestral colours to a pop or rock track

Usually you'll have other non-orchestral instruments taking up most of the frequency range available. If you try and fit a full orchestra into this you'll find that it probably overwhelms the other instruments in the track. There are a few things you can do to alleviate this situation.

Keep the arrangement simple. A small ensemble may be more useful than a full orchestra. Watch for any clashes with harmonies and don't use any bass string or low frequency brass instruments that muddy up the bass end. You may find that when you listen to the orchestral section in isolation it may sound thin and unrealistic; this isn't important – it's the overall sound of the track that counts.

Creating a more conventional 'orchestral-only' track

In this scenario, the orchestral library will be carrying the full weight of the recording. You'll need to use a more complex arrangement and instruments that cover the whole frequency range.

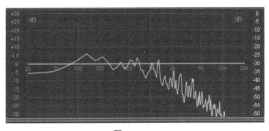

Frequency

Tip

If you have a plug-in that can display a frequency plot, insert this on your master output and you'll easily be able to see if you have gaps or bumps in the frequency range. A typical well balanced recording won't look flat; there'll usually be a bump at around 100–200kHz and a fall off towards the upper range. This is perfectly normal!

Tip

Run a piece of orchestral music through your plug-in to see what a 'real' orchestra's frequency range looks like

Figure 6.10
Frequency plot of a section of an orchestral recording.

Using the features of your orchestral library

Once we have a basic orchestration in our sequencer we can utilise the features of the Virtual Instrument plug-in to improve the realism of the score.

Finding the right sounds

Once you have the notes safely captured in your sequencer it's a simple task to loop around a part and select the sounds which fit the part best. Orchestral libraries often have complex names for each sound, such as SusLeg12Vln (which means a sustained, legato, 12 piece violin section), but these are usually abbreviations for the type of articulation and other parameters in the sound. While it's useful to listen to sounds in isolation, it's always better to hear the whole arrangement to see how the sounds fit. I'd recommend trying raw sounds and use EQ as a last resort if nothing you have seems to fit in the track.

Often, you can improve the realism of the orchestral part by using two different libraries in tandem and, for example, using the first violins from one library and the second from another. Another simple way of 'fattening' or warming up a string section is to copy the part to another track and add a warm string sound from a synthesiser and back off its level till it's almost inaudible. You can also add real instruments to the track – more on this later in the chapter.

Use the correct instrument

Although your sample library may allow you to play five octaves on a flute, don't be tempted to add notes which a real flautist could never play. Refer to the frequency/note range diagram in Chapter 4 (page 24) and, if you need to go lower than the flute, use the alto flute instrument – if you want to go higher, use the piccolo. If you need a more mellow tone, use the alto flute. If you want to add a bright and playful character, again, use the piccolo. Think of the best qualities of the individual instrument and what it is best at. Trombones can easily slide notes, trumpets can make you feel patriotic or exultant, French horns are muted and tubas can convey humour. Playing each sample manually should give you a feel for its suitability before you insert it in your score.

Articulations again

Acoustic orchestral instruments can be played in many ways, and the orchestrator will use these options to the full extent in a composition. When trying to create realistic orchestral scores you'll need to be aware of, and to use, these articulations in a way that's similar to the way in which they would be used in a real orchestra. If you just use, for example, a sustained string sound, it's likely that your score will end up sounding more like a synthesiser than real musicians. Articulations add dynamics and excitement to a score and also 'humanise' the recording. Individual libraries will vary in the number and style of articulations they contain, and it's a rule of thumb that the more expensive the library is the more articulations will be available. Here are a few of the most common you will come across along with handy guides to their uses. There can be as many variations of these as there are players of the instruments! It's up to you to decide what will best suit your music.

String articulations

Bow strokes

When a string player draws a bow across the instrument the sound of the up and down strokes are quite distinct and have quite individual tones. Players in a real string section will usually follow an up stroke with a down stroke – unless a specific effect is required. Some libraries also have variations on these themes – for example, by pulling off the bow at the end of the stroke. Players use these strokes to vary the dynamics between notes as well as within a single note. You may have to use the Expression MIDI controller to simulate the level changes a real player will insert into their strokes.

Figure 6.11
Using expression MIDI controller data to adjust the levels of notes and the dynamics between notes.

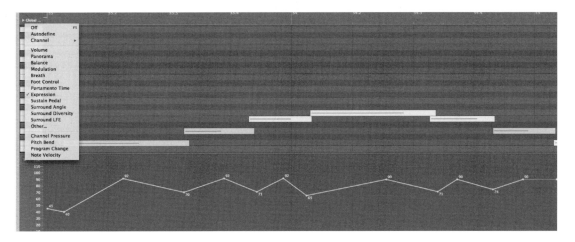

Attack

The way a bow hits a string has a profound effect on the sound. A strong attack will impart dynamics, while a slow attack can feel romantic, creepy or sensual. Swapping between the two give you a wide range of dynamic and emotional changes. In Figure 6.11 the attack of each note has been subdued using volume, but it's usually better to select articulations with less attack 'built in' if that is what you require for greater realism.

Trills

This effect entails the movement rapidly from one note to another and back again repeatedly. A sampled trill is always more realistic sounding than just playing the notes together on a keyboard, but obviously the speed and interval are necessarily fixed. Many libraries provide a selection of trills with varying speeds and note intervals.

Trills can lighten and excite when played at high pitches while adding drama and threat lower down the scale.

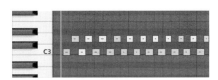

Figure 6.12
Trills between C and D.

Tremolo and vibrato

Tremolo is amplitude modulation (i.e variations in loudness) while vibrato is pitch modulation. Tremolo is the wavering between quieter and louder sounds while vibrato varies the pitch. When a string player wobbles a finger on a string, it usually produces a mixture of the two – but an experienced player also can control the balance of the two effects with their fingers. Both effects can be obtained in the synthetic library by modulating a sample's pitch or volume with a low frequency oscillator (LFO) – which allows for great control over the depth and speed of the effect. However, more realistic effects are obtained by using samples recorded with tremolo and vibrato – though you will obviously have no control over the effect and it may not 'sit' well in your composition. You can also sometimes use a LFO combined with a sample that already has the effect.

At high pitches, vibrato can sweeten and add emotion to a part. At low pitches, tremolo can add drama and menace to a piece.

Mute

A string player can use a 'mute' – a device which fits over the bridge of the instrument and, not unexpectedly, mutes the tone of the instrument. You can simulate this with a full range string part by cutting the high frequency portions of the sound using a filter or EQ, but a more realistic sound will always come from using muted articulations in a library. Muting the tone softens the part for romantic, pastoral or darker sections.

Slur and portamento

One of the benefits of string instruments is that, unlike a guitar, they have no frets. This means a player can slide up to a note (a slur) or slide seamlessly from one pitch to another (portamento). These effects can be simulated using 'standard' samples by using the pitch bend controller on your MIDI controller (or adding the data in your MIDI sequencer) – though some libraries supply slur and portamento articulations. Many plug-in libraries use the software's Portamento MIDI controller (MIDI controller number 5) to obtain the effect.

Slurs can add dynamics to the music while portamento can add a 'spooky' quality to the playing. Mixing in slow attack and slurs or portamento can create a build up to a section within a piece.

Pizzicato

This is the effect string players get when they pluck the strings. Pizzicato adds percussion and dynamics to a piece.

Staccato and legato

Staccato is playing in short, detached notes. Legato is the opposite, i.e. notes played in slow, smooth and connected manner. May libraries treat legato very seriously and it's looked at in more detail in Chapter 7.

Staccato adds speed and dynamics to a performance, while legato is more romantic and luscious.

Miscellaneous articulations

There are many other articulations which may or not appear in a library. Various methods of swoops, bowing, hitting, plucking and generally abusing the instruments can be found alongside many other extraneous noises players may make. Depending on the composition, these may add that extra bit of realism to a piece.

Brass and woodwind articulations

Many of the articulations found in these sections are similar to the ones found in the strings, such as Attack, Trills, Vibrato, Slides, Portamento and Staccato and Legato playing styles. However, as you may expect, the way the instrument is blown has as much of an effect as the way a string player bows their instrument. Using the tongue, players can add vibrato and fluttering effects and the velocity of the air entering the instrument affects tone and volume.

Percussion articulations

Percussion instrument articulations can come in an almost infinite variety of choices. Imagine a drum like a Timpani. You can hit it with sticks, mallets (made of different materials), hands and so on. Where you hit it changes the tone and attack qualities, as does the material the head and body are made out of. The choice you make depends on the music you want to produce and what your library provides.

Creating the score

Once you've decided which sounds and articulations to use, it's time to start to create your score. However, you should not see these choices as set in stone. As the composition progresses, you'll get new ideas and new additions will modify your choices. Don't be afraid to add or remove parts you think the composition requires. The final result is the only important thing, not the way it was achieved.

Creating sections – harmony and counterpoint

If you listen to any orchestral music, you'll hear that along with the 'main' melody there are often harmonies or other melodies complementing the lead. If you want to make your scores more realistic, you'll need to emulate these stylistic elements. But you need to strike a balance; too simple an arrangement may fit the song OK but may also sound synthetic; too complex an arrangement might overwhelm the song. Of course, if you're doing just orchestral work rather than adding it to a song, you can be more creative in your counterpoint and support melodies as you'll need to use these to generate interest, dynamics and power.

Here's an example of this. Let's take the simple arrangement we created earlier in the chapter. Here are the first and second violin sections.

Figure 6.13

In this case, both sections play the same thing, so let's change the second violin part. Use your sequencer's transpose function to lower the pitch of the second violin part by five semi-tones (i.e the first C down to G)

Figure 6.14

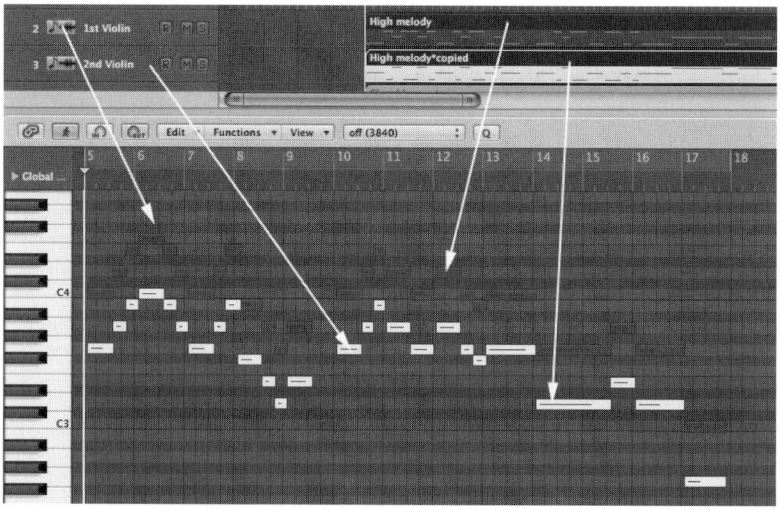

Now play this back. You may find that some of the notes don't quite fit now with the main melody, so you'll have to edit these individually. Just move them around until you hear something you like. If this is a part you're adding to a song, you'll need to audition it in the context of the overall piece to make sure nothing clashes with the orchestral section.

Now lower the level of the second violin part so it's just audible under the main melody. This gives it interest without taking away from the main theme. It's a subtle thing; too soft and it won't make any difference being there; too loud and it'll confuse the listener and take away attention from the main melody.

You can, of course, do the same with other instruments in the orchestra. For example, you may want the harmony to be played by clarinets or oboes for example. Brass instruments sound particularly nice when you have different parts playing different harmonies.

Harmony is an extremely interesting and important part of music making. Some harmonies fall better on the ear than others – which is why most music uses traditional two and three part harmonies. Common intervals are thirds (three whole notes apart) and fifths (five whole notes apart). However, which notes you choose are dependent on the key of the song. If you are familiar with keys and scales everything gets easier – but you can create interesting harmonies just by bringing the whole line down by three whole notes and editing any other notes that don't fit the melody. This method has one advantage – you're unlikely to produce 'text book' harmonies – which may or may not be a good thing! You'll soon get the feel for what will sound right and what will sound un-listenable – though, as in most art, there's nothing that's truly right or wrong – that's for the listener to decide!

Variety – the spice of the orchestra

DAWs make it very easy to copy and paste whole chunks of the composition to different parts within a song and it's always tempting, particularly if you are working to a deadline, to use this technique to quickly build up sections of your score. However, it's also the easiest way to kill any attempts you have made to make your recordings sound like a bunch of real musicians playing together! However, it still can be a useful addition to your compositional armoury if you bear in mind and apply the following modifications to the recordings:

• Change the actual notes in the different sections. Make each section slightly different, by changing the harmony, counterpoint or indeed main melody.
• Change the MIDI controller data. When you copy each section, you should also copy any MIDI controller data associated with it. Then you can easily modify parameters such as attack, timbre and any of the other MIDI controller-responsive parameters your sample library can respond to. If your DAW has a 'humanise' function, use this in a different setting on different controllers in each copied section.
• Change the articulations or the samples. In each section, modify the articulations at various points. For example, replace a sustained section with mutes, legato with staccato, try different slides or add some vibrato. You may want to swap the high string line with a flute or trumpet or blend the two together.

Adding the real thing

It may seem a strange thing to suggest in a book on creating music using a synthetic orchestra that you may like to use real players. But the addition of a single real violin playing the top line of the melody or a real trumpet playing the fast runs, can instantly increase the realism of the piece and fool the listener into believing that the whole piece is being performed by human musicians. Synthetic orchestral scores often fall down on the solo sections, so if these can be played by real musicians, it will really help to create a greater sense of realism.

MIDI and the score

A sample library on its own is pretty useless – some form of MIDI editing and playback system is also needed. Most DAWs have extensive MIDI editing systems and exactly which one you use is up to you – most modern software is up to the job of creating scores.

Entering MIDI note data – creating the score

There are basically two methods of entering the MIDI data into a DAW – using some kind of hardware MIDI controller, or by entering notes using the mouse, either as traditional notation or one of the other MIDI editing systems in your DAW.

MIDI controllers

These are usually keyboards or, less commonly, guitar, wind or percussion based instruments that send out MIDI note and other data. The notes are obviously used to enter pitch data, but the controller could also be used to send out other data that can be useful when creating a score, like that used to control volume, timbre or various articulations. These include:

- foot switches
- knobs and sliders
- ribbon controllers
- joysticks
- aftertouch and velocity

Wind based controllers, such as Yamaha's WX series also send out MIDI controller data that is affected by the blowing and the instrument can respond to tonguing and other breath control techniques. As you can imagine, these could be very useful for entering MIDI data if your library can make use of these specialised data.

Percussion controllers could be used to enter drum and other percussion instrument data.

Manual entry

If you have a background in music, you may want to use traditional notation to construct you score. There are several specialised packages designed with this in mind, some of which come with their own closely integrated orchestral plug-ins or packages. However, most of the more 'traditional' DAWs on the market are perfectly capable of becoming the centrepiece of a traditional notation based system. You just need to make sure that the package has a 'score' editor and that they have all the facilities you need

Figure 7.1

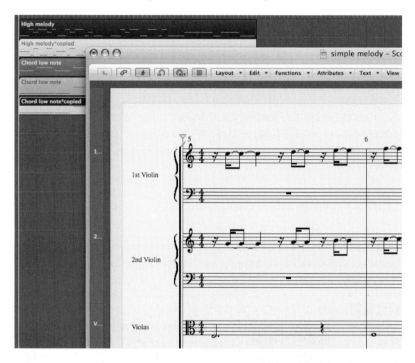

Figure 7.2

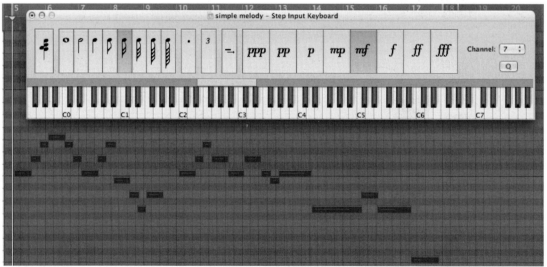

Even if you don't 'do the dots', you can use the sequencer's step entry system or other editors to enter notes using the mouse or computer keyboard. In some respects, this method of data entry is better than just playing the notes in from a controller – especially if you don't have much skill on keyboards. It's a more 'analytical' system and though it may take longer than real time entry, it will also stop any tendency you may have to play the parts as a keyboard player would – rather than treat them in an 'orchestral' manner.

Of course, you can combine all three techniques, real time, score and note entry – whatever suits your way of working best. For example, you may find playing in slow string parts is easier on a keyboard while complex passages are more suited to manual step entry. But of course, any errors you make can be easily corrected after the event.

Quantization

Many people think that quantization is only useful when generating music that adheres to strict timing, for example electronic, dance and so on, and that, as we are trying to produce a simulation of music played by real people it has no place here. But many DAWs now have intelligent quantization that can pull a performance into time along a defined grid or have 'groove' settings so you can simulate a particular feel, so don't ignore the technique.

Figure 7.3
Intelligent quantization can pull a
performance into time

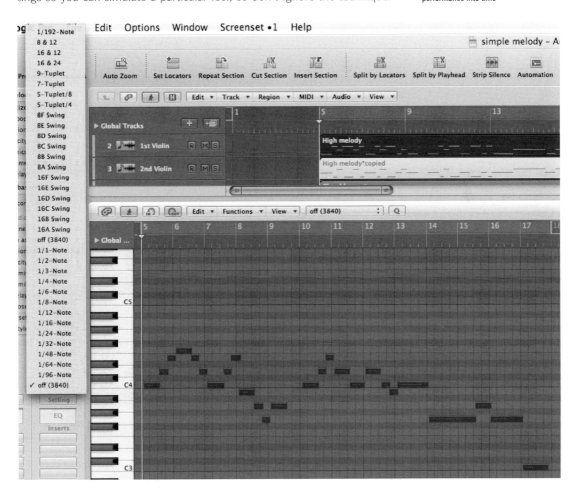

Copying notes and controller data

It's common when using a DAW to copy parts (along with any associated MIDI controller data) to rapidly build up sections of a piece. It's perfectly possible to do this when working on an orchestral score – but as we are trying to simulate the sound of a group of musicians playing together, you need to do some 'post processing' on these copies – this is covered in the editing section below.

Editing note data – editing the score

Once you have decided which articulations you want to use and have recorded the actual parts into your MIDI sequencer, there's plenty you can do to increase the realism of your performance. The MIDI editing side of a modern DAW is a powerful tool and you'll probably need to dig a bit deeper into MIDI editing than you are used to – you'll need to refer to Chapter 3 for more information about MIDI controllers and other MIDI-related information.

We've already dealt with the task of getting the note data into the MIDI sequencer. The way this data was entered will have a profound effect on how much editing you'll need to do 'post performance' and will depend on your skills at entering the data.

Editing the MIDI data

Most DAWs have a choice of editors for MIDI data. Most have some sort of Score editor, which allows you to add and edit notes using traditional notation.

Score editor

Even if you are happy using notation, there are still several advantages to using one of the other editors. It's usually hard to move notes around in time by small amounts and not all Score editors can display controller data alongside note data – which is very useful when you are trying to perform micro editing on the data.

List type editor

These types of editor display note and controller data as numbers and are extremely useful for fine tuning both note and controller data. However, it's often quite hard to understand what you are doing when you have no overview of the timeline – after all, music is all based on time.

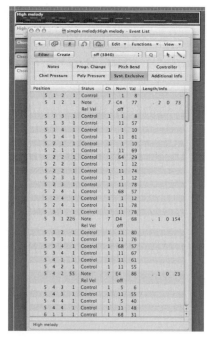

Figure 7.4

List type editor showing note and MIDI controller data.

Piano roll type editor

These editors display the note data as 'blocks' along the timeline. You can easily drag notes around and often you can can display many parts simultaneously (say strings, brass and flutes) and edit them all at the same time. Some piano roll editors allow you to also display controller data alongside the note data – especially useful as most sample libraries make great use of these data to control articulations and dynamics and so on.

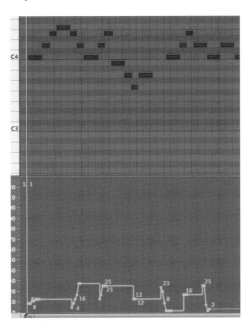

Figure 7.5
Some piano roll editors allow you to also display controller data a alongside the note data.

Info

Some DAWs allow you to run several editing windows in tandem allowing you to have, for example, a List and Piano roll editor open together and synchronised so that changes in one editor are instantly reflected in another.

Controlling articulations

The many articulations supplied with a sample library can usually be used in two ways.

Treating articulations as separate instruments

Using this methodology, each of the discrete articulations you want to use in a piece are loaded as if they were separate instruments. Say, for example, you've decided to use the following articulations;

- Sustained bowing
- Muted bowing
- Pizzicato
- Trills
- Tremolo

Figure 7.6

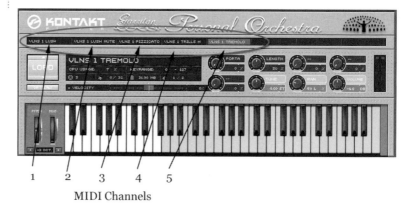

1   2   3   4   5

MIDI Channels

In this case, you might load each of these articulations into the Virtual Instruments as in Figure 7.6, each assigned to its own MIDI channel.

Now when these articulations are required, you simply place MIDI notes in the positions you want them to sound. In Figure 7.7, we have several notes of sustained playing, followed by pizzicato, mutes and trills a further sustained section and finally tremolo – all on consecutive MIDI channels.

Figure 7.7

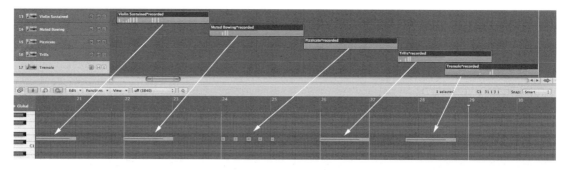

- Advantages: You can easily see where your articulations appear on the score just by looking at the editor.
- Disadvantages: Each articulation needs its own slot on the plug-in and you may have to use multiple instances of the plug-in to load every articulation you need. This could put quite a strain on your CPU and hard drive.

Tip

Figure 7.8

Start a note with sustained strings but end on a tremolo.

Using this method, it's possible to blend and crossfade between articulations. For example, you may want to start a note with sustained strings but end on a tremolo.

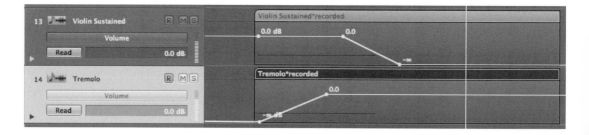

Using keyswitching

This technique is common in sample libraries and you'll find that there are usually 'keyswitching' versions of instruments. These use the MIDI notes (usually at the lower end of the keyboard) to switch on and off various articulations. The number and type of articulations available depends on the library you use. In this example,the following articulations are controllable from the keyswitched instrument by playing the respective notes first.

C   selects sustained violins
C#   selects mutes violins
D   selects alternate up and down bows
D#   selects up strokes
E   selects down strokes
F   selects pizzicato
F#   selects muted tremolo
G   selects tremolo violins
G#   selects muted half step trills
A   selects half step trills
A#   selects muted whole step trills
B   selects whole step trills

Figure 7.9

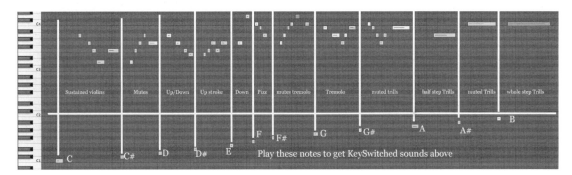

- Advantages: You need to load only one instrument to control several articulations.
- Disadvantages: It can be hard to keep track of what key is actually switching which particular articulation.

Info

Of course, it's perfectly possible to mix the two methodologies. You may have to do this anyway if your keyswitch instrument doesn't contain the articulations you need.

Controlling dynamics

Dynamics are the difference between the soft and loud parts of music. Real musicians use dynamics naturally when playing. The dynamic range of the orchestra is phenomenal and can alternate between a whisper and an ear-deafening roar. If you want to try and produce a score with realism, you'll need to make sure your score has plenty of dynamic range – where possible!

Some libraries allow you to control dynamics when you input the data in real time using MIDI hardware controllers such as foot pedals, sliders and wheels. This requires a lot of dexterity and it may be better to concentrate on entering just the notes first and worry about dynamics later – though you can, of course, modify the dynamic data later in your DAW.

Most libraries use two MIDI controllers to keep track of dynamics, Expression (MIDI number 11) and Volume (MIDI number 7). Both control the level of the audio but Volume is usually used to control the overall level of a multitimbral Instrument, whereas Expression controls the levels of the different element within that Instrument. So if you have eight different instruments loaded into your plug-in (violins, cellos, violas, trumpets, trombones, flutes, woodwinds and percussion) you control the overall level of all of these with the Volume controller while the balance of each individual orchestral sound within the instrument is controlled by the Expression controller.

Figure 7.10

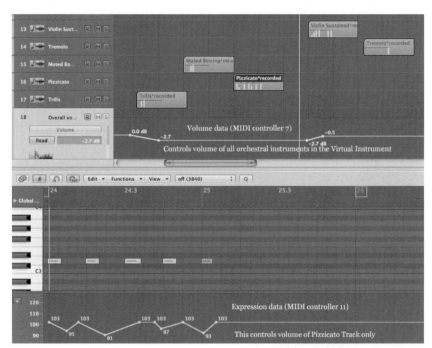

Some plug-ins convert the output of the Modulation wheel from MIDI controller number 1 to MIDI controller 11 as this hardware is easier to use to control volume than for example a slider or knob.

You can use Expression to control the dynamics of your individual parts. In Figure 7.10, MIDI controller 11 is being used to vary the relative levels of the different parts.

Cross fades
Although you can fade between articulations manually as described above, many orchestral libraries contain samples that can be cross faded internally using either a hardware controller (the modulation wheel is popular) or man-

ually using MIDI controller data in the DAW. These may allow you to fade between muted and bright brass or sustained and vibrato strings for example without using separate samples.

Some libraries also have so-called 'dynamic' cross-fades. With these, as you hit a key harder a different sample is played back. It could be, for example, that the string ensemble gets louder and brighter as you hit the key harder, or that muted strings are played at lower velocities while fuller, more open sounds sing at higher velocities. You can edit these velocities 'after the event' using your DAW to get the effect you want.

Controlling the timbre

The timbre (or tone) of the sounds you use plays a major importance in the way the orchestral parts fit in with the rest of your arrangement. For example, muted tones may work better in a song where there is a lot of bright-sounding material, whereas brighter parts may suit another song better. The best way to obtain the tone you want is to use samples which already have been recorded in a suitable fashion. However, most sample libraries also feature either simple tone controls (bass and treble) or sophisticated EQ or filters which can be used to adjust timbre.

Figure 7.11
Tone adjustment can be performed using either the Virtual Instrument or plug-ins on your DAW.

The importance of legato

When string players bow their instruments, they can either separate each note so they sound individually, or they can make them overlap and play seamlessly together. The former style is called staccato, the latter legato. Swapping between these two styles of playing will give your parts a more human feel and legato playing is the way strings produce their distinctive flowing style.

Sample libraries vary in the way they try and produce realistic legato style. Some allow you to switch between legato and staccato manually using a MIDI controller, and some attempt to analyse your style of playing and generate the style accordingly.

Miscellaneous noises off!

Human beings create a lot of extraneous noises when they play a real instrument. String players produce finger noise, scratches and even breathing can be heard in a strenuous performance! Brass and woodwind players generate key noise and all sorts of mouth-related additions to their sound that all contribute to the illusion persuading the listener that they are listening to a real player. If your library supplies these kind of articulations, depending on the kind of thing you are working on, they can add that little pinch of realism to your work. It may seem finicky and time-consuming, but it's these little details that can convert something from almost there to perfection!

Humanising the performance

When we use an orchestral sample library and a computer we are using a machine to make music. Machines are very good at precise, accurate repeatable performances. In comparison, real musicians are tardy, inaccurate, bad at reproducing repeated parts and often drunk! We need to dial back in this human element to our machine playback if we are to make our orchestral scores convincing. Before we can do this though, we need to decide exactly what real musicians actually contribute to a performance.

No one ever plays in really in tune

Many acoustic instruments are really hard to play in tune. Violins have no frets, while the pitch of brass and woodwind depends on the breath control of the players. When playing as an ensemble, these discrepancies create a lush rich sound as each tuning difference produce a chorus-like effect.

If you are using samples which consist of several players together in an ensemble, these discrepancies will be captured on the original recording. If you want to 'fatten' up these further, you could double up the parts with another, different sample. Using the same one twice will not create a fatter sound – perhaps the opposite, unless you de-tune the sample in some way. You can also use your plug-ins on your DAW or the library's own plug-in to add a gentle chorus effect to fatten up the sound and try and simulate these pitch discrepancies.

No one ever plays in time

If each note falls strictly on the beat, it's a dead give-away that real people are not playing the score. Some DAWs allow you to use so-called 'trans-

Figure 7.12
Use a plug-in or the Virtual Instrument 's
built in modulation effects to fatten up
the sound.

formers' to slip each note around on the timeline in a pseudo random pattern. These 'humanise' facilities, often also allow for the randomisation of other aspects of the performance, such as velocity (and thus attack), volume and other controller data. You could, for example, randomise the legato/staccato playing styles if your library allows these to be adjusted by MIDI data.

Humans adjust their playing depending on what the music needs at any given moment

There's no point in adding a full volume or dynamically varying score to a song if it's a subtle acoustic number. Part of this is in the arrangement, but also in how you control the dynamics of your MIDI playback. You need to try and think how real players would respond to the songs – after all, you are human too – and recreate this 'ideal' performance by editing of MIDI controller data and articulation choice.

Humans adjust their playing depending on how they feel

Whilst it's a cliché that orchestral players play a little more 'randomly' after a 'liquid lunch' I don't recommend you get drunk to simulate this effect! Just be aware that randomness and discontinuity is a part and parcel of a real musician's performance. Small additions of unpredictability and variability can pay dividends when attempting to simulate real musicians.

Enhancing the score

In Chapter 6 we started to construct a basic score which consisted of just the string instrument parts of the orchestra, violin, viola, cello and basses, along with the techniques which can be used to improve the realism and help to 'humanise' the score. If you are adding just orchestral colour to an existing song (but depending on the kind and complexity of score you wish to create), it can be enhanced further. A word of warning though; because most orchestral libraries come with an enormous choice of sounds and articulations, this doesn't mean you need to use them in every piece you write! Sometimes, simplicity is the key – especially if you are adding orchestral colour to an existing song. This is not always true of course – notably if you are composing a soundtrack to an action film, where often it seems like every possible articulation and dynamic is used!

Adding extra notes

As mentioned before, interesting and realistic orchestral scores don't consist of block chords where the notes change together exactly on the beat. The orchestral composer may add extra notes between chords to add interest to both the score and the players (if the score is being played by real players). Figure 7.13 shows a basic section consisting of the string parts of the orchestra.

Figure 7.13
A basic part consisting of the string parts of the orchestra.

We can adjust the exact point where the notes change to add some movement to the score (Figure 7.14).

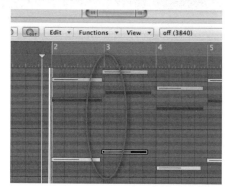

Figure 7.14

Next we can add some extra notes on the different part which lead neatly to the next notes (Figure 7.15). Next we can slur the beginning of the viola part slightly using the pitch bend MIDI controller (Figure 7.16).

Figure 7.15 (left)

Figure 7.16 (below)

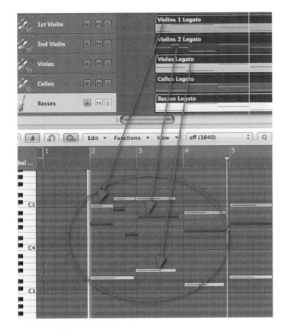 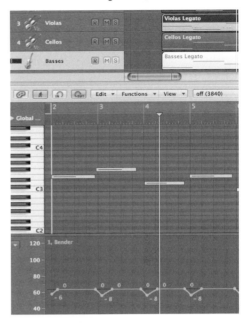

Then we use a different first violin articulation (staccato) for a few of the notes and a trill articulation at the end (Figure 7.17).

Figure 7.17
Use a different first violin articulation.

Finally, A few pizzicato notes from the cellos using a separate articulation (Figure 7.18).

Figure 7.18
A few pizzicato notes from the cellos.

The aim is to make the score varied as it progresses – just like a real orchestra would. Avoid copying verbatim whole chunks of the score or, if you must, adjust MIDI controller data, note start times, articulations and change a few notes here and there to differentiate the parts.

Adding extra instruments

So far we've only used a small section of the available instruments of the orchestra – though strings are by far the most commonly used – especially as an addition to an existing song. However, which instruments get used is really up to you. Many composer's styles are defined by their use of certain instruments in their scores, so don't be afraid to select whatever is needed for your song.

Brass

In some respects the brass instruments are often used as a 'section' in a similar fashion to the strings – i.e. the trumpets, trombones and other brass may make up the sections of a chord – so we can use the same techniques for separating out chords we used for strings in Chapter 6 (Figure 7.19).

Figure 7.19

Brass instruments can be used to create strident and powerful parts, but if you use muted trumpets or flugel horns or French horns, gentle parts can be created which can be used in the same fashion as muted synthesiser pads in an arrangement.

Brass instruments benefit greatly from using the available articulations and MIDI controllers to adjust attack and other timbral parameters. If you have them, adding flutters, trills, squeaks and other articulations can add interest and humanity to brass parts. You may also like to try detuning the individual samples; brass instruments are extremely hard to play in tune and the natural drift between players adds richness and warmth to a brass section. This is often captured in the recording of the sample but can be enhanced by using modulation or de-tuning samples against each other (Figure 7.20).

Figure 7.20

You can obviously use the same techniques outlined above for the string sections to add interest and a human feel to the score.

Woodwinds

By their very nature, woodwind instruments produce a more delicate sound than the strings and brass. They can be used to support these instruments, or be added to parts of the score where they are less prominent (Figure 7.21).

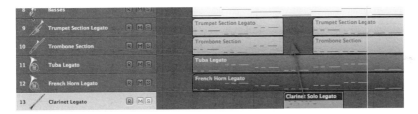

Figure 7.21

It's important to always keep in mind the way a real orchestra is laid out and the properties and capabilities of each individual instrument. For example, a group of flutes is never going to be as loud as a group of trumpets. You need to bear this in mind when composing for individual parts.

Because they are easy to achieve on these instruments, woodwinds are often given trills and grace notes to play.

Percussion

If you are adding orchestral colour to an existing song that already has conventional drums, you probably won't want to add cymbals, timpani and snare drums to the score. However, tuned percussion can often be used to great effect. Vibraphones could double up with or replace electric pianos, and marimbas or xylophones can be used to add rhythmic or percussive elements to a score. Gongs can be used to punctuate parts of a score, while bell trees can be used to add delicacy. Percussion can be used to enhance dynamics within a piece, and a cymbal crash is a common way to emphasise the end or start of a section. Orchestral drums usually sound quite different to their rock and pop counterparts, so can be useful in many situations. Depending on the samples you have available, orchestral libraries may contain all sorts of weird and whacky percussion instruments including coconut shells, shakers, bells and wood blocks. Whether these are of use to you depends upon the kind of score you are trying to create.

Keyboards

If you are adding orchestral colour to an existing song, it's likely that you already have a piano in there somewhere, but the harpsichord can be used to add percussive elements to funk or pop songs, while the pipe organ can add pomp and circumstance to a rock track or soul to a gospel or blues number.

Though there are many extremely good Virtual Instruments which finely sample every possible nuance of a piano, you may find that this is overkill when placed in the context of a score. The piano supplied with your orchestral library is likely to have been recorded with the intention of blending in with the rest of the sampled sounds, using similar recording techniques and ambience, and so may 'sit' better with the rest of the sampled orchestra.

More on quantization

We mentioned earlier that quantization, or the bringing notes into strict time, is usually the killer when trying to bring a 'human' element to a score. People never play exactly on the beat, so letting all your virtual players play on the 'dot' is not the best way to create realistic scores! However, most DAWs have quantization tools which can help in getting a performance that is 'tight' but not 'robotic' – which can be really helpful if you are entering notes manually in real time and your playing abilities are not up to scratch.

Choose the correct quantize value

If you have a piccolo playing every 16th note in the bar, there's no point in choosing a quantize value of 1/8th notes! You need to select a value that closely resembles the parts you are playing. Your DAW may also allow you to select compound quantize values (such as 8 and 12, which corresponds to eighth and eighth triplets being quantized) and unusual values such as 7 or 9 time. Don't worry too much if you don't understand the musical terms – nearly all DAWs have undo features and quantization is almost always changeable in real time so you can see how these different choices affect your score. Quantization values usually are in reference to a grid set on the DAW transport bar (Figure 7.22).

Figure 7.22
Un-quantized playing.

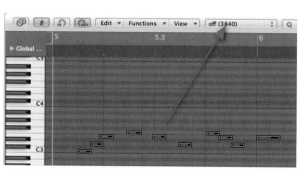

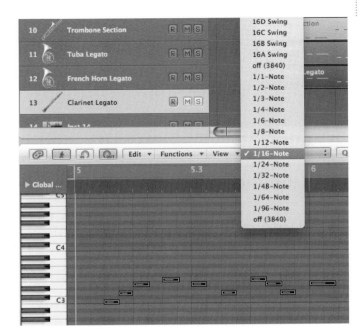

Figure 7.23
Quantized to 16ths.

Quantize strength

This parameter allows you to adjust exactly how much the MIDI data will be affected by the quantize value and how close the notes will be to the grid (Figure 7.24).

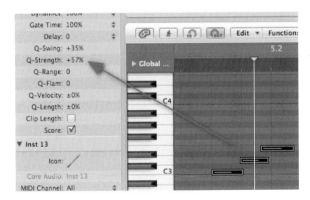

Figure 7.24
Adjusting quantize strength.

Quantize sensitivity or quantize range

This parameter defines what MIDI data around the grid will be affected by the quantization. At high values, all notes are affected, but reducing the value means that notes further away from the grid line are not affected by quantization.

Quantize swing

This parameter (Figure 7.25) moves notes in reference to each other rather than to the fixed grid. This allows for a looser feel to a recording – which may or may not be what you are after!

Figure 7.25

Groove quantize

This technique usually entails taking a recording you like the 'feel' of and creating a MIDI file using the DAWs audio to MIDI facilities. Then, you create a Groove template from this file and apply it to your MIDI data. The Groove usually appears in the list of available quantization values, so it can be adjusted using the different quantization techniques described above.

You'll probably find that percussive elements of your score respond best to quantization. But don't be afraid to experiment!

Some DAWS will have more adjustable parameters you can adjust to get you feel 'just right'.

Tempo and time signature

Quite a lot of modern music has a fixed tempo – i.e. it remains the same speed from beginning to the end. In fact, it's quite surprising just how many contemporary songs are set to tempos which are multiples of the resting heartbeat – i.e. 120 beats per minute (twice the resting heartbeat) being extremely popular. Human players are not like this; they vary tempo throughout a piece of music, slowing down slightly for a build up, speeding up in a chorus or solo, slowing down at the end and so on. Classical music is full of

Figure 7.26

Tempo changes occur frequently in classical music.

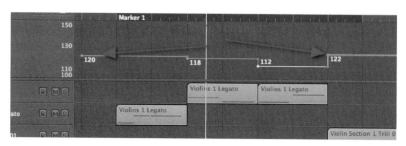

tempo changes, some of them surprisingly large, but you can also use tempo changes successfully in a more contemporary setting by varying the tempo at various positions throughout a song.

Note that while MIDI data (and thus Virtual Instrument data) can easily follow any tempo changes you insert, your DAW may or may not allow already recorded audio files to follow these changes.

Time signatures represent the number of beats in a bar. Most DAWs default to 4/4 time (four beats in every bar) but don't be afraid to experiment with other signatures. 3/4 time can impart a waltz-like feel, while 5/4 time can add a jazzy flavour. It is possible to 'mix' time signatures within a piece. For example a four on the floor (4/4) dance song could incorporate a section of strings in 3/4 time – they will meet up every three bars of the 4/4 time (4 x 4 beats in three bars=12 beats total, which is the same number of beats as four bars of 3/4).

These compound times are very popular in 'world' music and can add rhythmic complexity to simple backings.

Mixing

Mixing is the process where all the elements of the orchestral parts are blended down into a seamless and, hopefully, realistic whole. How much work you need to do here depends on how much mixing you have been doing along the way. It's natural when composing and sequencing to balance the different instruments which go to make the orchestra so they sound 'right' as you go along. It's tempting with multi-output Virtual Instruments to send each instrument to its own mixer channel and treat them differently with EQ and reverb just because you can. But we are trying to produce the impression of a bunch of musicians playing together in the same place, so isolating them is kind of counter productive. It's also why it's better to use different instruments and articulations to adjust the tone rather than process them overly in the plug-in window or using your DAW's EQ plug-ins. What this section does not cover is mixing in general; the information here is specifically for your orchestral parts.

It doesn't matter which DAW or which computer platform you use to mix your orchestral piece. The samples in this chapter mostly feature Apple's Logic Audio DAW and The Apple Macintosh computer – but all the tips are equally do-able in most DAWs which accept VST, AU or RAST plug-ins.

What are we trying to achieve?
Though the orchestra can be seen as a single large instrument, there are some considerations that need to be addressed when mixing a track.

Basically you'll be working in one of two ways:

- Producing an isolated orchestral piece or ensemble section that needs to stand on its own.
- Producing an isolated orchestral piece or ensemble section that needs to fit in with a song or other material.

Both these aims have many similarities, but there are also some different approaches that we need to be aware of when mixing.

Getting started

It's likely that you may have a multitude of orchestral Virtual Instrument tracks in your composition. Figure 8.1 shows a typical layout – though you could have many, many more tracks like this depending on the number of

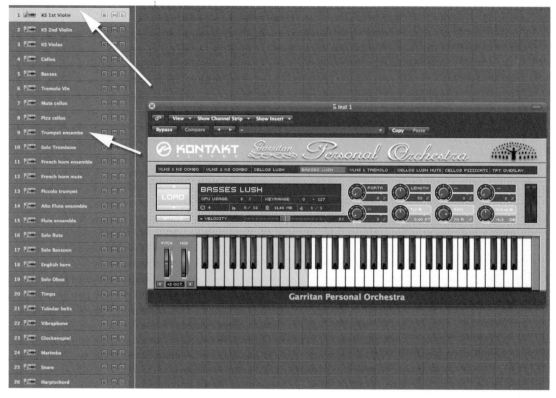

Figure 8.1

Figure 8.2

articulations you want to use. The piece here makes use of keyswitched instruments which contain many articulations, but some 'extra' ones have also been added.

For example we have keyswitched first violins (a sample made up of 12 violinists), keyswitched second violins (a sample made up of 10 violinists), keyswitched violas (a sample made up of 10 viola players), cellos (eight players), basses (seven players), tremolo violins, muted cellos, pizzicato cellos, trumpet ensemble, solo trombone, French horn ensemble, French horn mute, piccolo trumpet, alto flute ensemble, flute ensemble, solo flute, solo bassoon, English horn ensemble, solo oboe, timpani, tubular bells, vibraphone, glockenspiel, marimba and snare. Oh, and a harpischord!

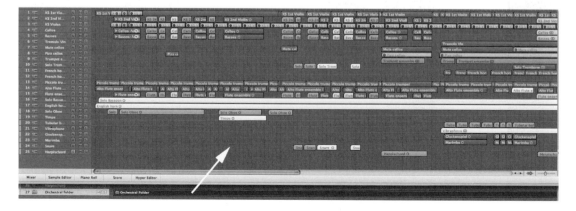

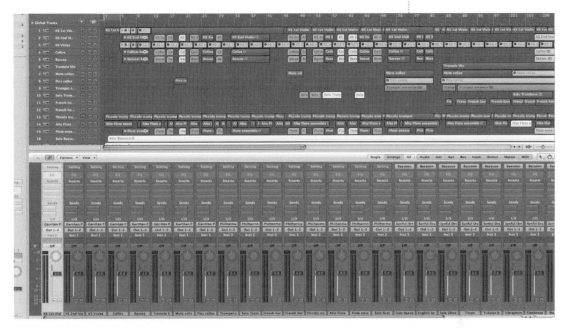

That's 26 actual tracks – and the number of players represented depends on the number recorded in each sample! As you can imagine this can lead to confusion! If your DAW supports it, it's often a good idea to pack your tracks into a folder, rather like the operating system folders on your computer. This means you can treat the whole of the orchestral tracks as if they were just one single track (Figure 8.2).

Figure 8.3 shows the tracks laid out in the DAW mixer page. Note that different parts are being covered by different Virtual Instruments.

In Figure 8.4, each orchestral track is part of an 8-part multitimbral instrument. Having a single individual Virtual Instrument for each orchestral instrument often makes it easier to balance the sections, add any effects and maintain the relative balance of the individual parts. The disadvantage is that this method will grab more CPU cycles. Using a multi timbral instrument is more efficient, but potentially more confusing and harder to process each part separately in some DAWs

Figure 8.3

Figure 8.5
Output diagram for each track having its own Virtual Instrument.

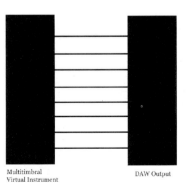

Multitimbral
Virtual Instrument   DAW Output

Figure 8.4
Using Virtual Instruments in single and multi-timbral mode.

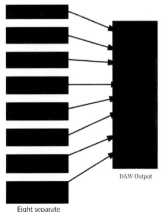

DAW Output

Eight separate
Virtual Instruments

Levels

Mixing is, above all, about balancing the levels of the various aspects of the orchestra. How this is done will depend on the two criteria defined under 'What we are trying to achieve' earlier in the chapter, but the idea is to make sure that the levels of the instruments fulfil the following;

- They have a good internal balance and nothing sticks out or important parts are not audible.
- They have a good balance with any other aspects of the composition.

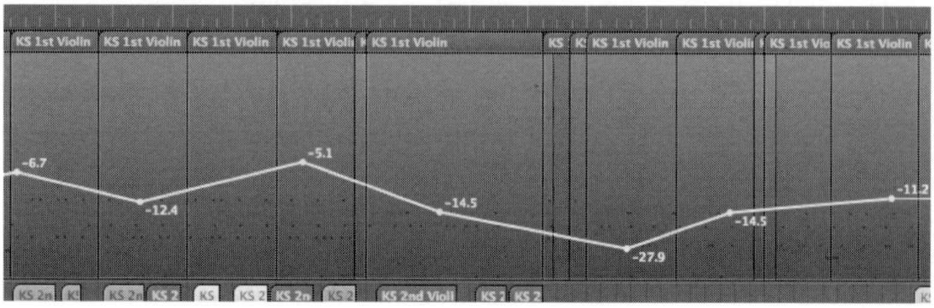

Figure 8.6
You can use your DAW'S volume automation to adjust levels in the same way you can use it to vary MIDI controller data.

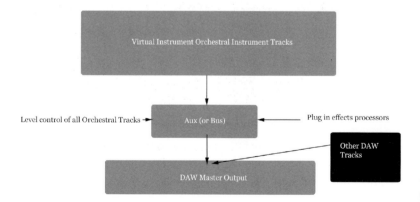

Balancing is done by adjusting the level of the faders. Some DAWS allow you to group faders together so when you move one of the group the others move keeping their relative positions.

Figure 8.7
Some DAWS allow you to group faders together so when you move one of the group the others move keeping their relative positions.

However, I'd recommend that you send the tracks to another channel, called an AUX (or a BUS) in most DAWs. This is a specialised channel which is then routed to the main output. You can then use this channel to control the overall levels of all the tracks passed through it.

Figure 8.8
Routing through an AUX (or BUS) track.

Virtual Instrument Orchestral Instrument Tracks

Level control of all Orchestral Tracks →   Aux (or Bus)   ← Plug in effects processors

Other DAW Tracks

DAW Master Output

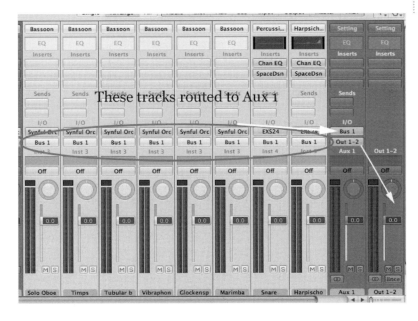

These tracks routed to Aux 1

Another advantage of this scenario is that it's easy to add an effect such as reverberation or EQ to all the tracks together (Figure 8.10). This can help to 'gel' the individual tracks together. More on this later in this chapter.

Position

Unless you have a small ensemble or are looking for a special effect you need to position the different instruments as a listener would hear them in a concert hall. If you refer to Figure 4.5 in Chapter 4, you can use the Pan control on your DAW tracks to position them correctly on the soundstage.

Figure 8.9 (left)
Aux (or Bus) track

Figure 8.10 (above)
Adding effects to several tracks
simultaneously.

Pan controls

Figure 8.11
Pan your tracks for optimum positioning
in ther soundstage.

Some libraries provide stereo or surround sound samples which already have their position 'locked' into the recording. If this is the case, it's best to leave the Pan controls set to the centre position.

Figure 8.12
Send tracks to a reverb plug-in.

In a stereo recording we perceive depth by hearing acoustic reflections from distant instruments in a different way to nearby ones. You can simulate this by adding an AUX (or BUS), inserting a reverb plug-in on the AUX, and sending different amounts from individual tracks depending on their position. For example, you may send more of the distant brass than the closer strings. You'll need to experiment with these levels, but you don't need to add much reverb to make a difference before the individual tracks start sounding too isolated.

Tone

Tonally, each part should sound as if it fits in with the other parts and also does not stick out from other elements of the composition. The best way to achieve this is to use the correct samples – if you need a more muted tone, use a muted sample. You can do so much with EQ, but each part treated with too much EQ can start to sound unnatural and get us away from the very effect of realism we are trying to achieve.

Effects and the mix buss

Because the tracks are all sent through a single AUX (or BUS) it's easy to use this track's fader to balance the whole orchestral part against other elements of the song. You can also easily add effects here too. The most useful are detailed below.

Reverberation

Reverberation is the effect you get in a room which has hard surfaces (often mistaken for echo, which is actually discrete repeats). Reverberation or Reverb is a more diffuse effect, consisting of complex early reflections followed by a decay. Adding reverb to the whole of your tracks can give the illusion that they were all recorded in the same space – adding to the realism. Which reverb you use is down to taste and the effects you have available. Modelled or Impulse response reverbs contain samples of real acoustic spaces, many of which have actually been used to record orchestral pieces.

It's important not to use too much reverb as this will increase the sense of distance – although this may be exactly what you want!

Info

Some libraries come with reverb recorded alongside the samples which can either be 'dialled in' at various levels or are fixed in the recordings. It's worth trying these samples first. They may not be as flexible as a plug-in reverb, but are probably best used if you are after the ultimate in realism.

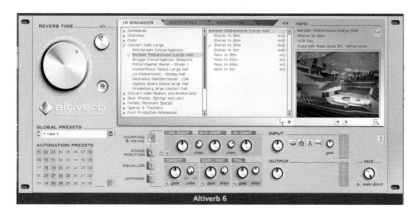

Figure 8.13
Reverb is a diffuse effect, consisting of complex early reflections followed by a decay.

Equalisation (EQ)

EQ affects the tone and, as was stated earlier, it's best to choose individual samples carefully rather than use EQ. However, using an overall EQ to sculpt the whole orchestral performance can be used to fit it in better sonically alongside other elements in a track or to boost specific frequencies to add power or weight. Often it's better to use an EQ which has broad sweeps rather than one that can hone down to specific frequencies accurately. Emulations of classic EQs are particularly useful here especially if you are after a specific effect. Perhaps you could use an emulation of Abbey Road EMI EQs if you're after that Beatles vibe?

Figure 8.14
Use EQ to sculpt the whole orchestral performance

Figure 8.15

Info

The Virtual Instrument plug-in used for a library may contain its own EQ and effects. Often, they do not sound as nice as the ones that come with or can be added to your DAW, but they often are very CPU efficient and can be useful if you have to add effects to individual instrument tracks.

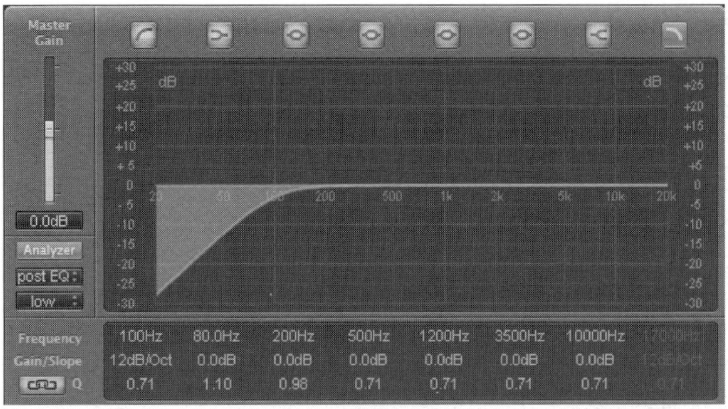

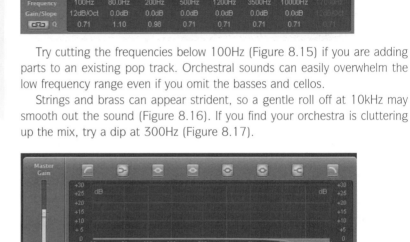

Try cutting the frequencies below 100Hz (Figure 8.15) if you are adding parts to an existing pop track. Orchestral sounds can easily overwhelm the low frequency range even if you omit the basses and cellos.

Strings and brass can appear strident, so a gentle roll off at 10kHz may smooth out the sound (Figure 8.16). If you find your orchestra is cluttering up the mix, try a dip at 300Hz (Figure 8.17).

Figure 8.16

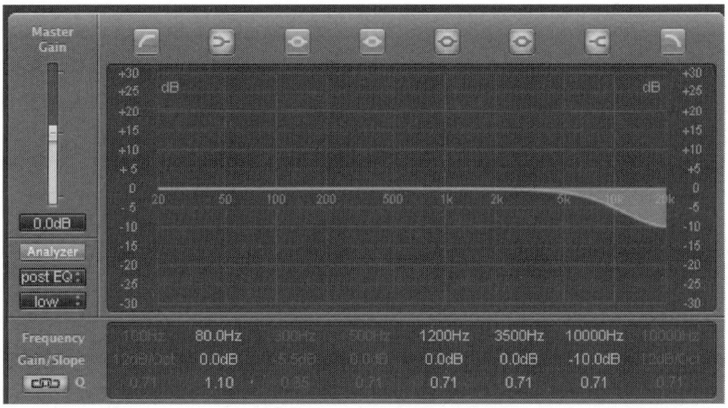

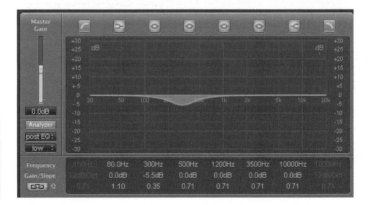

Figure 8.17

Tip

Try not to boost the frequencies too much. It's always better to cut the problem frequencies in other parts of a track.

If you find the orchestra is not cutting through, try a wide boost around 10kHz (Figure 8.18).

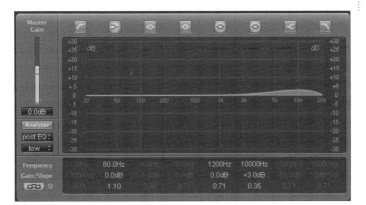

Figure 8.18

Compression

A compressor squashes the dynamic range of a signal and is commonly used to make sure different elements of a recording are not too loud or quiet. Orchestras have a large dynamic range and compressing them too heavily can make them sound unnatural – something we wish to avoid! However, a splash of compression can 'glue' the orchestral element together and ulti-mately into a song. Using a classic emulation can often add a certain 'sound' as they colour the tone in specific ways.

Try a gentle compression with a ratio of 2:1 and a fast attack and a 0.5s release. You'll have to experiment with the attack and release controls as you don't want the compression to be obvious. Pull down the threshold control until you have applied the effect you want.

Figure 8.19
A compressor reduces the dynamic range of a signal.

Special effects

Once you have your orchestral composition sounding as realistic as possible, don't be afraid to add special effects. Pop music in particular often uses phasing, flanging, chorus or more wild and wonderful effects on whole string sections and orchestras.

Mastering

Mastering used to describe the process of preparing a tape recording for cutting onto vinyl. Mastering engineers, with many years of experience under their belts, would prepare the tape with specialised equilisation (EQ) to allow the recording to be squeezed onto the disc with maximum fidelity. With the advent of CD and digital recording, Mastering has come to mean something quite different.

Mastering may involve any or all of the following processes:

- Arranging each piece in the correct order (compiling) if you are producing a work containing many songs or sections.
- Matching the level of each song or section so that there are no jumps in volume between them.
- Fading in and fading out the songs or sections, or using crossfades if you want them to blend into each other.
- Processing with broad range EQ, compression and limiting to add a professional 'sheen' to the recordings and to make them sound more cohesive when listened to as a whole or when comparing them against other recordings.
- Creating a Master CD-R from which you can produce normal audio CDs or further CD-Rs.

Mastering is often seen as a kind of arcane art. However, modern audio recording software and DAWs offers us the facilities to produce our own masters, using the same tools used for mixing. Listening to your own CD collections is a good way to hear what a good mastered recording should sound like in comparison with your own work.

You will often hear people say that you cannot do your own mastering – you really need to send your mixes to a specialist. While it is true that there are many talented people with esoteric equipment available at high cost, it really is possible for you to master your songs yourself. Mastering isn't magic; it's like any process of recording. You need to practice, experiment, listen and try and fail before you get a good 'ear' and become proficient in the various techniques.

You are unlikely to have available an acoustically perfect room for mastering your work. So you'll need to become familiar with the room's quirks. Listen to lots of commercial CDs in the room you'll be mastering in and compare these to your own efforts. With care, you'll be able to adjust your mastering technique to produce similar high quality work.

Tip

Leave your mixes for a while before you master them. It's always a good idea to lose some familiarity with the work – you need to try to look at it as if it was a new recording.

Info

Re-mastering is the process of taking old recordings and using digital technology and plug-ins to improve their sound for CD production.

You may want to master each song or section separately and then arrange them into the correct order afterwards. This may also be a useful method if you are using plug-ins that require a lot of CPU power.

Most of the tools you'll need are exactly the same as the ones you have used when mixing. A large portion of the mastering process will entail the use of these plug-ins.

The type of mastering processing required will depend on the recordings themselves. Even if you have recorded and mixed all the songs in a similar fashion, you'll find that they probably vary quite a bit in volume and tone.

Adjusting the level
You can use your audio software's automation to level match the recordings. If you listen to a few minutes of the end of one track through to the first few minutes of the next, you'll get an idea of the relative volume levels. You can then adjust the track levels using volume automation.

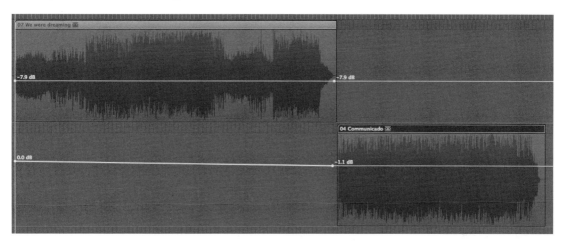

Figure 8.20

If you want track fade-ins and fade-outs you can use volume automation for this as well (Figure 8.21).

Figure 8.21

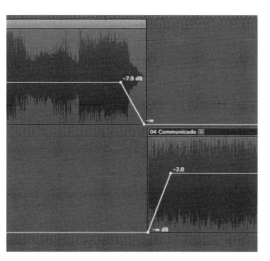

Figure 8.22

Crossfading from one track to another is also possible using volume automation.

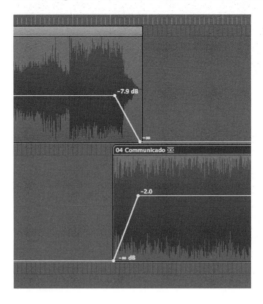

Processing

Next, we'll want to process the songs or sections with plug-ins. You don't always have to do this; processing isn't always needed. You may find that the mix sounds exactly the way you want it to as it is.

However, most mixes will probably benefit from processing. You don't necessarily need to use all these plug-ins on every track. You'll need to make some creative decisions when listening to your recordings.

Remember to keep bypassing the plug-in(s) to hear the effect they are having on the songs. Processing, especially boosting frequencies using EQ, will often increase the overall volume. This increase in level can easily be mistaken as a 'better' sound. Try to keep the processed and bypassed sound at the same level using the plug-ins mix or level controls.

Mastering tools

Compression

You may want to use compression (Figure 8.23) to 'level' out the volume changes of a completed and mixed piece. Many compressors have a 'sound', which they will impose on the recording. Some compression plug-ins simulate valve or classic compressors, which again have their own specific 'sound'.

Orchestras can have a large dynamic range. Compression will reduce that range so use them sparingly for maxim realism!

The problem with compressing a whole track is that one element of the sound, say the bass drum or cellos, may trigger the compressor in a way that isn't suitable for the rest of the track. You may find the track 'pumping' or distorting in some way. Gentle compression is usually needed here.

Info

Whether you process, using the EQ first or the compression first is a debatable point. You can experiment with both ways and see which works best for you.

Figure 8.23
Compressor.

It may help to use these settings as a starting point.

Ratio
Try a compression ratio in the range 2:1 to 5:1

Attack
Set this to 2ms or 'fast'. This means the signal is affected quickly – i.e. the compressor works right away to keep sound level in volume.

Release
Set this to around 0.5s. You'll need to experiment with this value. Too slow a release will make the sound unnatural.

Threshold
Turn down the threshold control until the compressor starts to work (you'll see the actual gain reduction in the meter on the compressor). Further reduce the control until you get a nice level sound.

Gain make up
Increases the value of the gain make-up control until the compressed sound is at the same level as the non-compressed one.

Multi band compression
One way to get around the problems with 'normal' compression is to use a multi band compressor (Figure 8.24). This splits the audio stream into many frequency bands – usually 3 or 4. The frequency ranges of the bands are variable and each band has its own compressor. The idea behind multi band compressors is that you can affect the various frequency ranges in different ways. For example, you could compress the higher frequency range which

Figure 8.24
Multi band compressor.

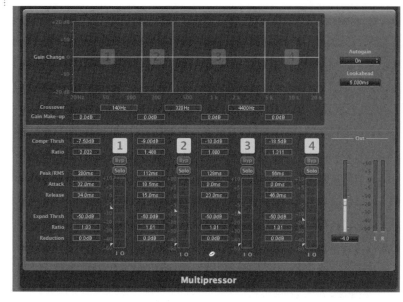

contain the strings more than the cellos or bass, or select a narrow frequency range to correct and reduce the level of excessive scratchiness in violins.

Some multi band compressors allow individual threshold levels to be adjusted along with an 'overall' one. You can usually 'solo' each individual frequency band to hear the effect on that band alone.

Multi band compressors are complex beasts by their very nature and the parameters available may vary. However they usually come with a range of presets to get you started.

EQ or equalisation

Whereas during mixing we were often using EQ to correct and enhance the tone of individual instruments, when mastering it's a more gentle correction that is required. You may want to subtly enhance the high frequencies or reduce or enhance the bass.

Figure 8.25
Equalisation.

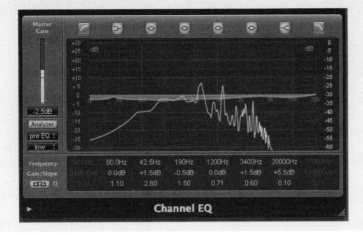

As usual, the EQ you use is going to be dependent on the type of record-ing you are mastering and the result you are trying to achieve – but here are a few settings to try as a starting point.

- Boost a few dBs at around 15000Hz to add 'air' to the track – but watch for sibilance (loud 's' sounds) or excessive high frequency unpleasantness – this is particularly important if you are using violins or trumpets, for example.
- Boost at around 80Hz to enhance the low end.
- Cut at 300Hz to remove muddiness. Don't be tempted to use too much boost or cut.

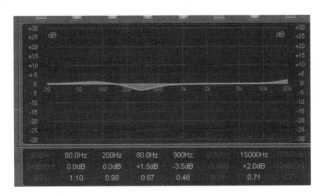

Figure 8.27
EQ settings to try as a starting point.

You may want to use a 'classic' emulation of EQ and/or compression to enhance the overall 'tone' of the mix.

Figure 8.28
United Audio UAD-1 Pultec EQP-1A software EQ

If you find that you are boosting or cutting frequencies by a large amount to make the recording sound OK, you should consider re-mixing the song.

Limiting or maximising

Limiting is the last effect you should use in the mastering chain. It's a severe form of compression which stops the output going over a certain pre-set level. This will allow you to push the volume as high as possible without hitting 0dB and digital distortion. In addition, limiters often have the facility to pull up low-level signals, thus compressing the sound into a narrow volume range. These limiters are often called maximisers.

Figure 8.29
Limiter.

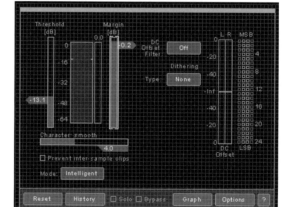

There is a trend to use limiting to obtain the loudest volume and song energy as possible. While this type of mastering may sound OK on an FM radio, it does usually produce audible artefacts and can be harsh and tiring to listen to.

To use a limiter for mastering try the following settings as a guide.

- Set the output level to –0.5dB. This means that the level will never go above this value.
- Depending on the limiter, either push up the gain control or reduce the threshold to increase the overall volume of the song. This has to be done by ear. You'll see how much gain reduction is being applied in the meter (Figure 8.30).

Figure 8.30
Meter shows increase in gain.

Other mastering effects

While the above are the 'classic' mastering effects, you may also like to try some other plug-ins to enhance your songs.

Exciter

This is a specialised plug-in that applies EQ, distortion and compression to make the sound more 'present' and brighter in tone. Exciters can initially make things sound very impressive – but they may be wearing on the ear after a while, so be careful how you apply them.

Figure 8.31
Exciter

Valve or tape emulators

These plug-ins add a 'warmth' to the sound. Overused, they can make things sound woolly and muddy.

Reverberation

Though you would usually use reverb on individual instruments or sections when mixing, there are time you might use it over a whole song or piece. For example, if you are trying to make give the impression that the drums, band and string section were all recorded in the same location, you may apply a small amount of reverb to the whole song. Convolution reverbs which use

Figure 8.32
United Audio UAD-1 DreamVerb
software.

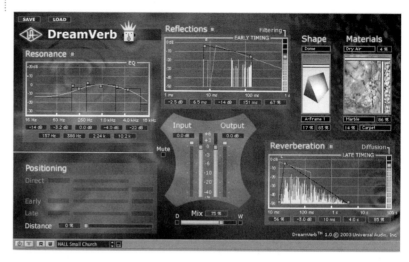

recordings of real locations as the basis of their effects are particularly useful for this purpose.

You need to be careful adding reverb to a whole track though. An almost inaudible amount of reverb can add a kind of audio 'glue' to a track, but adding too much can make it sound as if it was recorded in a church – which is, of course the effect you may be after! For subtle reverb, choose a short room preset and add the effect until it's just audible, then back off on the control a bit. The reverb decay time and pre delay can have an enormous effect on the final result so it pays to experiment.

Using the above tools will help make the orchestral sections added to a song 'fit' better and a also help make orchestral-only recordings sound more 'coherent' – both these effects will help with perceived realism of the orchestral arrangement.

Figure 8.33
Audioease's Altiverb convolution
reverberation

Producing a score for real musicians

Although producing an orchestral score within the computer using an orchestral library can produce results which, under certain circumstances, can be easily be mistaken for the real thing, there comes a time when a composer may wish to, and have the budget to, record real players. Not only does this produce excellent results (assuming you can get musicians of the required standard) but the experience is also extraordinarily useful for when you come to produce your next synthetic score. If you take note of the way the players interact and play your parts, it should help you with your next project – particularly if you isolate the individual sections in separate tracks and can listen at your leisure to how the performers play.

While this section doesn't cover the actual physical mechanics of recording an orchestra – that would take another, completely different book, it does suggest some ideas to make your recording sessions more successful, efficient and above all, fun!

The score

You can't just print out the tracks you've created on your DAW and expect musicians to play the the parts note-perfect. You will have modified your computer performance to sound right when played back by the computer – but this won't necessarily make it read correctly for a musician. Take the following piece (Figure 9.1). It's a simple string part played into a DAW and assume that on playback it sounds exactly the way you want it to.

Figure 9.1

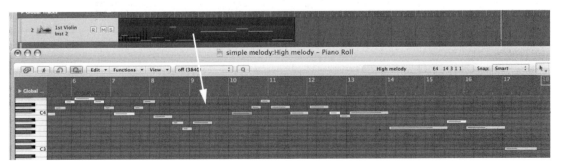

Now here is the DAW's interpretation of the part in the score editor.

Figure 9.2

I think you'd find it pretty hard to get a musician to follow that! Traditional notation can only be an approximation of a performance. Written notation is 'quantized' in a way, and performance and other denotations of the style and emotional input into that performance are added afterwards. So if we use the quantization on the DAW we can make the part look like this.

Figure 9.3

Tip

It''s probably better to work on a copy of your piece. Then if you still have a 'playback' ready copy to refer to.

This is much easier for a musician to follow, but will not sound right when played back by the computer – which of course is not important! Your DAW may also have 'interpretation' or 'style' features which can help in placing the part correctly on the stave.

Info

Your DAW may have score-editor only quantization and interpretation tools which can assist you to produce a more readable score.

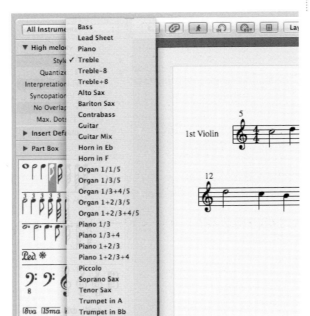

Figure 9.4

Transposition

One of the most confusing aspects of producing a score for real orchestral instruments to play is that many of them need to have notes on the page that aren't exactly the notes that will sound from the instrument – meaning that the notes they play are actually different from the ones written down. A clarinet player playing a Bb instrument, would actually sound a Bb when reading a C on the page. The reason this came about historically is to keep the notes on the staves rather than have a lot of sub staves.

This can cause confusion when printing out a score for instruments such as clarinet, trumpet French horn and some piccolos. Some Instruments themselves give an indication of the transposition needed – i.e. Bb trumpet, whereas others do not. Luckily, the DAW score editor usually allows you to

Figure 9.5

choose (or create) an Instrument style for a particular part, so the printed part will correspond both to the notes you expect to hear and the notes the instrumentalist expects to see in the score.

Common transposing instruments

- Clarinet is usually a Bb instrument. The most common clarinet sounds one whole tone lower than written, so parts for it must be written one whole tone higher than concert pitch. So a written C will be played as a lower Bb.
- Trumpet and cornet can be in Bb or C (written C is played as a C), depending on the individual instrument, but Bb is the more common key for cornet.
- English horn is an F instrument. A written C is played as a lower F.
- French horn parts are usually written in F (i.e a written C would be played as a lower F).
- Alto flute is in G (written C is played as a lower G)
- Some transposing instruments do not change key, but play an octave higher or lower than written.
- Guitar parts are written one octave higher than they sound.
- String bass parts are written one octave higher than they sound.
- Piccolo parts are written one octave lower than they sound.
- Contrabassoon parts are written one octave higher than they sound.

The instruments that transpose an octave have either a very high or very low range. Transposition puts their written parts comfortably on the stave.

The musicians' skill levels

While your synthetic score may contain parts of great dexterity, you may find that the musicians you have to work with are not quite as skilled as your computer at playing them. Be prepared to modify your parts to fit the abilities of the musicians. It's always better to use a simple part well played rather than a complex part badly played. You need to use your communication skills and talk to your musicians to gauge their confidence.

Working with the players

Unlike the computer, which (mostly) does what you tell it, musicians are human beings with all their strengths and weaknesses. Most people like to be involved in a process and they often get more out of it if they feel they have really contributed to something special.

When you hand each player (or group of players) their parts, encourage them to read through the part and make notes and questions. Getting them to rewrite out their parts, means that they should pick up any problems in the score, such as notes un-playable on their instrument or require an impossible technique. Discuss with them the emotional impact you wish your piece to make, where crescendos should occur and any other dynamic you wish to impose upon your music. It's likely that your score won't contain enough of these indications to guide the players – getting them to rewrite your score will allow them to write these things down. If you collect these notes after the recording, they can provide an invaluable account of how real players like to annotate their scores, which will be really useful in later sessions.

Make sure the musician's version of the score has the same bar numbers as your synthetic one – this makes it easier to pick up at different sections of the score as it's unlikely that you'll be playing from bar 1 each time!

Remember, a musician who is good enough to play your score will have years of experience with their instrument. They are the experts, not you! Listen to their suggestions carefully and implement those you think may enhance your score. However, don't be intimidated; you are the composer and the musicians are used to deferring to the wishes of the composer.

Conducting the session – being there

Unless you are an experienced conductor, I suggest either getting in someone to conduct (the leader of the players you have hired may be able to suggest someone or may decide that one is not needed if they will be playing along with a DAW). Rather, your role is to listen and suggest if things are not sounding the way you want.

- Make sure the musicians are playing what you want. If not, stop the session and explain to them more clearly or play back your guide music.
- Listen out for tuning discrepancies. If you hear anything is off, don't be afraid to ask the musicians to check their tuning.
- Listen out for strident or out of place instruments. Though you can fix things 'in the mix' to a certain extent, problems like obtrusive E strings on violins, can be almost impossible to subdue when mixing. If you hear any problems like this, try to isolate them and correct them at source.
- Watch where the string players are playing your notes. For example there are many positions on the violin, for example, where you could play any given note. However, the tone of the different notes can vary, with lower strings generally being warmer in tone than the higher ones. Also, pitch slides and swoops are easily done on the same string, whereas jumping to another string will make these impossible. These little slides are part of the 'certain something' which can convert a performance into something special.

Doubling the parts

If you are on a budget and have a smaller ensemble than you'd really like (i.e. you really want 22 first violins and you could only muster 5) consider doubling up the parts. You could either get the whole ensemble to play along with a track several times, or even just the sections you require to make the sound fatter. You could, for example, record the brass section only once, but the strings three times. Bear in mind though that if you are paying by the hour, it may be more economic just to hire enough players. Also, musicians may not play each subsequent run through as well as the first.

Bringing a recording along to the session

If you bring along a CD or MP3 of the synthetic score, you can refer to this as the session progresses or, indeed, play sections of it to the musicians if they are unsure of your wishes at any point.

Adding synthetic parts

Once you have captured your performances of your score with real players, don't be afraid to add sections of your synthetic score alongside the recordings. Though this wouldn't be done in a 'classical' recording, it's fairly common in popular music to underpin sections with synthetic instruments to add power and weight, or even to keep a 'feel' you may think has been lost in the recordings of real players. It's always tempting to use everything you record at an orchestral session, especially as it's likely to have cost you money, but the final product is king; use only what you need to get the results you want.

Re-using the live playing – record everything!

An orchestral session can be a rich source of useable material apart from the actual notes you use in your score. You could, for example, use sustained sections to create your own string samples, use noises made by musicians before they start to play to add realism to a synthetic score or sample the brass section's initial attack to add realism to your synthetic ones.

Appendix 1
Glossary

Analog(ue)

With respect to audio signals, analogue refers to a continuous waveform, as opposed to a digital one that is described as a series of steps.

Amplitude

The 'loudness' of an audio signal.

Audio interface

This is the hardware that allows audio to be input and output from your computer. It could be as simple as the stereo in/out card or built in soundcard or as complex as a multi in and out system with extra DSP processing.

BPM (beats per minute)

The tempo or time of a piece of music.

Bit

The smallest unit of digital information described as a '1' or a '0'.

Buffer

A portion of computer memory that stores information before it is read to and from a hard disk. A buffer basically speeds up hard disk recording.

Byte

An 8 bit binary number. A kilobyte is 1024 bytes, a megabyte is 1024 kilobytes and so on.

Clipping

Clipping occurs when audio levels exceed 0dB. This is a bad thing. You should not exceed these levels unless you deliberately want to make your audience's ears bleed.

CPU

The 'brain' or Central Processing Unit of a computer.

DAC

Digital to audio converter. Converts digital data to analogue data.

dB

Decibel. Unit of loudness. Decibels are a logarithmic scaling, so that a 3dB drop in level equals a 50% loss in signal strength and a 6dB reduction is a 75% loss in signal strength.

Digital

With respect to audio, digital signals are made up of discrete steps representing analogue waveforms. For example if you sample an analogue waveform at 44.1kHz you will have 44100 steps every second. The amplitude of the waveform is described by the number of bits. CD is 16bit, 44.1kHz digital recording. In general the more bits and the higher the sample rate, the more accurately the digital representation of the analogue waveform.

Di box

Simple hardware device to allow the outputs of guitar and bass to be matched to a line level input.

DSP

Digital signal processing. Term used for any audio feature that uses the computer to emulate hardware units such as synthesisers, effects units and so on. DSP can be done either using the computer's main processor or additional external DSP chips, depending on which audio interface you have.

Editor

A window within a sequencer where you can edit MIDI data.

EQ or equalisation

Equalisation is basically a process of tone manipulation. EQ can vary from simple bass and treble controls to sophisticated multi-band parametric models where you choose a specific frequency to be cut or boosted.

FireWire

Similar to the USB 2 protocol. Used to connect external devices to a computer.

Hard disk

A device in a computer which stores programs and data.

Hertz (Hz)

Unit for measuring frequency. It describes the oscillations per second.

Line level

Signal level produced by the audio outputs of equipment such as CD players and synthesisers.

Mic (or microphone) level

Low-level signal produced by microphones. It needs to be amplified by a pre-amplifier to a line level before it can be recorded.

MIDI

MIDI stands for Musical Instrument Digital Interface. This was first established to allow the connection of two or more electronic musical instruments. This serial communication protocol has gone on to become the method of interfacing keyboards, computers and a wealth of MIDI devices and has become one of the most enduring 'standards' of modern times. MIDI data is also used when recording and playing back Virtual instrument plug-ins.

MIDI channel

MIDI devices send and receive data on up to 16 MIDI channels. These are not to be confused with the number of tracks a MIDI sequencer can record on which can, on modern computers, be almost infinite. Well a pretty large number anyway.

MIDI clock

A timing message embedded in the MIDI data enabling instruments such as drum machines to keep in time with another MIDI device, such as a sequencer.

MIDI controllers

Either the MIDI data used to control the parameters of a Virtual Instrument or the hardware device which generates the data.

MIDI message

The data passed between MIDI devices. MIDI messages can be note data, controller data, SysEx data and the like.

Multi timbral

The ability of a synthesiser or module to produce several different sounds on different MIDI channels at the same time.

Plug-ins

Third-party software that runs inside audio music software. Plug-ins can be software recreations of existing musical hardware, such as synthesisers or effects units, or completely new programs. Plug-ins can be of many different formats depending on the computer and host software, such as RTAS, VST and AU.

Quantizing

Quantizing is 'bringing into time' unruly audio recordings or MIDI note data. It's used, for example, to bring drum parts into time. Quantizing can be used as a creative or restorative tool.

RAM

The memory in a computer where programs are run when they are loaded from hard disk. RAM stores data temporarily and all data is lost when the computer is switched off.

Real time

Performing an action along with the natural flow of the clock. For example, if you bounce down a 4 minute track to a WAV file, it will take 4 minutes to complete the bounce.'

ROM

The permanent memory in a computer that runs essential operating software.

Sample rate

The number of times per second an analogue signal is measured in digital conversion.

Signal to noise ratio (S/N)

The ratio of signal level to noise level in an audio system expressed in dB.

Soundcard

See Audio interface.

S/PDIF

Sony/Phillips Digital Interface. A low cost option digital interface. Similar to AS/EBU but using phono connectors.

Step time

Entering MIDI note data with the sequencer stopped, a note (or chord) at a time. See Real time.

USB

Universal Serial Bus. Computer interface protocol for external devices. Comes in two speeds USB 1 and the faster USB 2

Virtual effects and virtual instruments

Software recreations of hardware equipment or completely new programs that run as plug-ins within audio music software.

Appendix 2
The internet

The software and hardware used for orchestral simulations is continuously in a state of flux. New products are appearing all the time, so we've provided the following Internet link to enable you to keep track of what's new in the field.

www.pc-publishing.com/orchestration.html

This link provides pointers to various manufacturers' websites, useful mailing lists and Internet fora dedicated to the art of using computers to produce orchestral simulations. The links will be updated regularly, providing a one-stop resource that is always up to date.

Index